The Changing Culture of Libraries

The Changing Culture of Libraries

How We Know Ourselves Through Our Libraries

Edited by RENEE FEINBERG

McFarland & Company, Inc., Publishers
Jefferson, North Carolina, and London

Library of Congress Online Catalog Data

The changing culture of libraries : how we know ourselves
   through our libraries / edited by Renee Feinberg.
      p.   cm.
      Includes index.
      ISBN 0-7864-1138-4 (softcover : 60# alkaline paper) ∞
      1. Libraries—Aims and objectives.   2. Libraries and society.
   3. Libraries and community.   I. Feinberg, Renee.
   Z716.4.C+   2001034248

British Library cataloguing data are available

Manufactured in the United States of America

Cover image ©2001 Art Today

*McFarland & Company, Inc., Publishers
   Box 611, Jefferson, North Carolina 28640
      www.mcfarlandpub.com*

In recognition of the changes in my life, my retirement from
socially responsible work as a librarian at Brooklyn College,
and in recognition of the changes in my family life,
the marriage of my daughter, Sheelah to Andrew,
and the death of my father, Boris:
I labored with this book in respect and fondness for the students
and faculty and staff of the City University of New York
whose mission of access and excellence in higher education
for New Yorkers keeps me in awe.

Renee Feinberg
Winter, 2001

"America why are your libraries full of tears?"
—Allen Ginsberg, "America" *Norton Anthology of Modern Poetry* (1973), 1126

Acknowledgments

Writing projects require tremendous support from friends, colleagues and institutions. I was particularly fortunate to have this support. Professor Geraldine DeLuca edited the manuscript and Professor Jocelyn Berger lent her skills in desktop publishing. The Professional Staff Congress, the union representing faculty and staff, provided a small grant.

Table of Contents

An Introduction: Libraries in Tears

Few of us writing for this collection would consider ourselves professional writers. Most of us are practicing librarians with a point of view and a passion: we care deeply about our libraries and our communities. We have come together in this volume to wrestle with what we think needs to be said about libraries and our role in them. Many found it difficult to actually put pen to paper and to avoid duplicating the usual formulaic library article, well researched and hortatory. What we have attempted to do is to reflect on our having spent our professional lives as librarians as well as to explore the changing nature of library service as it is transformed by the revolution in cyberspace.

Most of the authors in this collection share my views on pro-active library service and social responsibility. I hope that by assembling a congenial group of librarians, library users and library sponsors who weathered the evolving nature of my demands for a certain kind of essay, I could rely on them to express—in their individual voices—my personal vision. But it seemed unfair not to accept my own challenge, and so I struggled with this introduction. If this book is my swan song and the bookend to a long career, surely I could find something to say which was both personal and political.

What is it, then, that I want to say about libraries and to whom? As an academic librarian, I have spent a good deal of my professional life in an ongoing discussion with administrators about our curricular responsibility, which for libraries is mostly about how we identify the needs of our students and how best to meet them with the resources we have gathered to make available in the library. This dialogue has often sounded more like an airing of agendas than the articulation of a vision. But it's time to move beyond such stalemates and express my aspirations for my community, in this case, an academic urban community of poor and working class students many of whom are immigrants and people of color. I think I feel strongest about enticing young people to the world of books, and to the pleasures of reading. I envision young people reading and being read to; and I conceive of reading not just as a pleasure but as an obligation for all who aspire to be both concerned and cultured citizens.

Unfortunately, I find that many Brooklyn College students do not read for pleasure. As young adults, their experiences with books have been with expensive textbooks, which increasing numbers of them tell the reference librarians they are unable or unwilling to buy. Many of our students do not have discretionary funds to experiment with buying books: to choose them, smell them, enjoy them, share them, get crumbs in them, mark them—all the things one does not dare to do to the more public books from the library, or should I say, did not dare to do at one time.

It would have been a wonderful mission for librarians to have turned students on to books, to building their own libraries, to diminishing the sense of remoteness that has come to dominate our libraries, due to either the hauteur of museum-like buildings or, at the opposite end, the tawdriness of Brooklyn College's library, which is under renovation. I think that, as a group, librarians have failed to turn students on to a book culture that is both pleasurable and rewarding, glorious and seemingly infinite. And we continue to fail to encourage students to explore their way through our libraries' collections so that they might challenge their personal opinions and expand their knowledge.

Ideally, we should have tendered our mission more closely and made students more welcome to the world of books, a much more profound and mysterious and self-guided world than the Internet ever could be. However grandiose and whiz-bang the Internet may be, it holds less mystery and personal discovery. Jumping from cyber-link to cyber-space seems contrived and less creative—how unlike a book journey which takes place in one's mind where the trail is unlinked and unmarked, where the only partner is the self, and the only obstacle is one's desire to continue or not.

The Struggle

I fear that librarians are losing the struggle to hold on to the history and the traditions of a book culture, which are the foundations of a liberal arts education. Toni Morrison writes: "Access to knowledge is the superb, the supreme act of truly great civilizations. Of all the institutions that purport to do this, free libraries stand virtually alone in accomplishing this mission" (4). This sense of mission to educate and to bring the gifts of civilization to the public is not new to libraries. Jennie Flexner of New York Public Library expressed similar views almost a half century ago. Though she could be called an elitist, she sought to use the library and her individualized reading lists to improve the downtrodden and unfinished immigrant. She also put the public libraries on the map as institutions that would serve people. And in so doing, she and those of us who come after her, pledged commitment to making book collections available to people not so much for the moral uplift, as to bring pleasure and introduce people to that special exchange between librarian and reader.

In remembering when she signed up for her library card, Vivian Gornick writes of that silent signal which passed between her and the librarian which seemed to say: "We are keepers of the culture, you and I. The book is everything. We're here to respect it." To introduce people to those pleasures which librarians know intimately was really how libraries claimed us as people who were to spend our professional lives working in them. We have known deep personal satisfaction reading and visiting libraries. How very sad, then, that we now become those who watch as libraries become forbidding places that are tending towards the disenfranchisement of the community.

The City University of New York

Today, the City University of New York is under siege by our legislators and politicians to reduce the power and prestige of an historically great urban university. While under siege, librarians have been unable to hold on to the ideal of the book treasures in our libraries. We have failed to maintain the collections we inherited from previous generations and to pass on stronger collections. We have failed to articulate what we know to be true and no less important than the literacies we hope to teach our students, the taste for books. We have failed to communicate the pleasures of confronting knowledge, of possessing a book, of engaging it in a way that is private and deep, fundamental and democratic.

As I review my more than 30-year library career, I find that while I was vague about my career choices, I was adamant about working in New York City. Having grown up in an affluent community, I saw nothing appealing about working in other well-heeled communities, so I taught in the New York City school system. I chose teaching, as well, because it appeared to be a meritocracy and I could be hired without having to please the interviewer; however, I suspect this was less true than I thought because applicants were indeed screened for a host of reasons, I suspect speech and appearance among them. I left teaching because the classroom seemed to be a lethal box barely containing the angst and hostilities of teens and teacher.

I began library school in the heady days of 1968 when attending classes and getting arrested in antiwar demonstrations seemed compatible. I was enthusiastic about my political activity and I understood our shared behavior to be an important part of the larger peace movement and a tough birthing of our generation in an adversarial relationship with authority as well as a commitment to a mobilized citizenry for social change.

In the early '70s, I became a school librarian in a Brooklyn school district which was newly organized under the decentralization movement that gave the community control of the schools. Once again political forces were strong, but I wasn't clear how to respond professionally in order to take advantage of the political situation. Were we to attend meetings with parents, march on the Board of Education or change the reading lists? Eventually, I migrated to an urban college because I was unable to find a niche for library service in the public schools that went beyond arranging books neatly on shelves and overseeing children who read quietly for a class period. Then in academe the demands of faculty status, research and publication kept me buried under obligations which thwarted whatever activism I thought myself capable of. And I suspect that child care responsibilities further drained the development of social awareness.

As I got older and had fewer institutional and familial demands, my political activism blossomed again. As a feminist, I now find myself participating in a re-energized rank and file union movement. Like other writers in this collection, I doubt whether my activism changes anything about my library work except to make clearer to me how much I detest a hierarchic workplace where notions of managerialism seem to promote unilateral decision-making as a substitution for collegial articulation of programs and dedicated library service.

The struggle to hang on to our curricular responsibilities and our sense of civic mission during times of budget cuts and the uneasy transition to the "electronic library" leads me to think that we have lost our way. I suspect that there is a general unease among many librarians as we review changes in library service driven by the new technologies and reduced funding. We have been ill-prepared to fight budget cuts. We have not been engaged in the dialog to reassess values of service and we have caved in very early in the struggle. Since these struggles come at a time of relative peace and prosperity, we have forgotten that the greatest struggles are often lost when we are prosperous and at peace. We have snoozed while the strong-arm of catch-up and consumerism has engulfed us, and we have some bad choices in our libraries.

In her critique of the Benton Report, Kathleen de la Peña McCook notes that we assume a rosy future for libraries with the same equanimity that we are accepting the prosperity of the country as the stock market continues to be bullish. There is, she says, "seeming unilateral acceptance of the digital onslaught. Print collections were built with care and selectivity over decades, but digital information systems seem to be heralded as an unquestioned solution to all information needs" (626–28).

Books

As I witness the destruction of library collections, I note the managerial impatience with print, the resentment and disparagement of information that can't be electronically accessed and printed offline. I find library literature full of discussions of pieces of the larger social and library picture. I read about the Barnes & Noble and Borders bookstore wars with smaller stores reported from Los Angeles to New York City; the continuing underfunding of children's libraries and collections; the struggle against censorship. I read about exorbitant serial pricing structures and the struggles by library consortia to confront this. I also read about authorship and copyright issues. The discussion of these substantive and heady issues leaves me wondering who is minding the store and ensuring that our libraries continue to be accessible to our communities?

Over time I have not changed my belief in the fundamental importance of reading, writing and numbers mastery, and the ability to apply these disciplines to reading a book. Book reading requires reading a physical book and the time, the quiet, the privacy, the space, if you will, to withdraw into another place that is absorbing, provocative, reassuring, touching, or whatever we wish, accompanied by the physical experience, the smell and feel of books and the pleasure in moving a lamp, clearing off a chair, chasing the kids away. These are themselves significant parts of finding the time to read.

All of this assumes some leisure and choice. We are concerned about time: we talk about how time has speeded up. In the City University, our students "have no time." They work, they parent, and they attend college. They have few opportunities to reflect, to read, to muse. Stanley Aronowitz of the City University Graduate Center comments that we are training our students, not educating them: education takes time.

I guess that bypassing the book culture in our educational routines allows us to communicate to our students that public life is easy in this democracy, that it doesn't require contemplation or preparation and study. All we need is information delivered to us privately to enable us to make our choices. Unfortunately, most of the choices we are making these days are consumer choices: we shop for doctors, airline tickets, or the latest gossip. We are—no matter the chat rooms—bowling alone. We no longer encourage our students to associate reading books with learning. We encourage them to log-on and print-out and catch the train, the class, the job, or pick up the kids. We do not encourage them to consider how time-intensive education is and how demanding is its handmaiden, book reading.

As practitioners we seem to be participating in a new kind of ghettoizing. It's not that our communities will be left behind in the latest technological revolution, but that they will be left behind intellectually because we have signed on to the technological bypass that leapfrogs a book-based culture. Those who rely less on public institutions will continue to read and enjoy books. They will be an elite group who have been taught the value of reading a book as one of the hallmarks of a cultured, well-regulated life. With relative peace and prosperity in this country, we need to think about these inequities and strive to make sure that leisure and disciplined thought are secured not only for the wealthy and privately educated.

What, after all, is computer literacy? Is it working the keyboard? Is it finding your print-out? Is it finding the assigned site? Is it surfing the Net? Is it e-mail? Is it providing for those who have limited physical vision? Is it making sure that the universe of electronic services, both fee-based and free, is available to all much as we made books and journals available? Certainly, libraries are promoting ready access to more online information than anyone needs in a lifetime. As Wall Street has said, "Anything with a dot com is it." And so say all the current pack of Mac-billionaires. Should we sign on? I have no problem with any of these literacies. They just seem rather slim compared to the literacies of time, space, thought and reflection encouraged by reading books.

The Library

My concerns with library work come from my work at Brooklyn College whose culture seems faddish and insidious. It values a business model of management where flashy consumerism has come to represent the bottom line of library culture. To deliver the product most efficiently, library management, both locally and university-wide, advocates a uniformity at both ends, conception and delivery. It is to their advantage that we downsize and homogenize and commodify. Information becomes a rigidly controlled market product. Never mind the democratic features of the Internet. The means of productivity, if you will, are heavily controlled by telecommunications monopolies with the support of the federal government

It is not the technologies that upset me. What I find to be destructive of time honored library traditions and library values is the way we have chosen to embrace change. This managerial culture we have allowed is seduced by the hucksters of the "dot.com" culture. In its rush to be online and ontime, management sweeps away the foundations which support strong and accessible book collections and bibliographic expertise. As management does not engage in conversations with the librarians most involved with service to patrons, we see a surprising re-enactment of the folktale about the emperor having no clothes.

Contributors

The original call for papers asked writers to consider the uniqueness of their work and their service commitments to their communities. As conversations proceeded between the editor and the contributors, the call changed to allow for personal essays which have a political note. I hope readers will find in this collection some heroes who struggle to preserve something of our traditional library culture until a time comes when the currents of the ideology of the book and preservation of book collections are stronger.

While many of us writing in this collection report of our struggles, others do not. But we have all struggled with our writing, for it was my intention to gather together practitioners who seldom appeared in print. Many who have contributed to this collection were willing to grapple with the discussion but found the discipline of inward-looking difficult. All the authors were encouraged to write about their experiences through the lens of their career choices, often their lifetime choices: What does it mean to have spent much of our adult lives working in libraries? What does it mean to imagine spending a lifetime as a librarian? What people have said here places us, I suppose, all over the map and that's a good thing. The need to understand what abandoning traditional library values means to us as professionals and to our patrons, perhaps, can be captured as we write about ourselves. How else to engage in understanding the destruction of our library traditions?

Works Cited

Gornick, Vivian. "My City: Apostles of the Faith That Books Matter." *The New York Times* February 20, 1998: E2, 43.

McCook, Kathleen de la Peña. "The First Virtual Reality?" *American Libraries* 24(7): 626–628.

Morrison, Toni. "Intellectual Freedom." *ALA Action* (1998) No. 2:4.

Why Library School?

Tony Doyle

Tony Doyle is currently a reference librarian at Hunter College of the City University of New York.

When I was poised to attend library school in the fall of 1996, I knew it wasn't going to be pretty. I was in it strictly for the piece of paper, which is more like a union card than a certificate of academic achievement. I knew too that this was going to be very different from real graduate school, where I had studied philosophy. Librarian friends warned of sheer drudgery.

Graduate study of philosophy had its frustrations, like graduate school generally. I made my way through with a teaching assistantship. Like non-unionized grad assistants everywhere, I was egregiously underpaid; I didn't even have a place to meet with students outside of class. Add to this a course load of nine credits a semester and you have an almost leisure-free life. And more than a few of the professors were arrogant and aloof. A couple were simply jerks. But most were learned and highly intelligent; many were inspired teachers. It was *philosophy* that kept me and my peers going, and that was a lot. We were all passionate about the discipline, reveling in discussions of it around the philosophy office or over a few beers on Friday afternoon. Graduate school was sometimes irritating and always demanding, but often exhilarating and generally rewarding.

Library school could hardly have been more different. It was all that I'd expected and probably worse. Sure, I had some good teachers—three actually. Two were librarians, one recently retired; the other was an archivist. Their years in the field were their greatest asset as teachers. My other teachers were—library scientists. They styled themselves "doctor" and assumed professorial airs, notwithstanding having no real discipline to profess. For the first couple of months I felt as if I had walked into some bad parody of academic life. Needless to say there were no beer-soaked Friday afternoon colloquiums devoted to various theories of the reference interview or the benefits of the 1956 edition of the *National Union Catalog*.

The general atmosphere was like boot camp. The "professors" often addressed us as if we were obstreperous conscripts. The average age of the students was probably mid to late 30s. Most had worked for a living for years; many, perhaps most, worked in libraries. Nevertheless one professor was forever reminding us that we were now in "graduate school" and that we were responsible for coming to class prepared and getting our work in on time, as if we didn't have to meet deadlines in our professional lives, as if we hadn't when we were undergraduates.

The classes themselves, excluding those taught by the capable teachers mentioned above, were dreary beyond description, particularly the introductory ones that I took my first semester. I'm no advocate of distance learning; I strongly suspect that it's just correspondence education for the digital age. However, I left nearly every class with the sense that my time would have been better spent at home. Take General Librarianship, which for some reason was required. The earlier part of the course dealt with library history; later we allegedly learned about the current state of libraries and librarianship. The teacher was probably the worst I've ever had. Each week he would dust off another stack of transparencies consisting of his "lecture" notes, evidently unchanged for twenty years. Then he would proceed to read haltingly from these, adding very little more content. Nor did he have any sense of how to conduct classroom discussion; he seemed incapable of responding appropriately to student questions and comments. This went on excruciatingly for the first two thirds of the semester, after which he kicked back for a parade of student presentations. It was actually a relief to get a break from his pedagogy. From what I could tell the teacher did nearly no class preparation for the balance of the term. And he certainly knew how to lighten his grading load. The course requirements consisted of two computer graded multiple choice exams, the aforementioned presentation, and a five page paper, which he returned nearly comment free. Nice work, I thought, this being a library school professor. Where do you apply?

Another required course was called something like Technology in Libraries. The instructor was a bitter and irascible man who generally enjoyed bullying and intimidating students. The course, so far as I could figure out, was mostly about computers. At any rate the lectures—ramblings really—had mainly to do with computers, and the text was called *Living with Computers*. Yet the course itself was bizarrely hands-off. Not once in class did we put fingers to keyboard. And there was virtually no required computer work outside of class. There weren't even any computer demonstrations, though for some reason one evening our teacher gleefully dismantled an obsolete personal computer before our eyes and passed the components around, identifying them as he did. Why? Beats me. The course included two baffling projects. One was pompously called "visual literacy." It required that we paste ten postcards, united by a common theme, onto a poster. Memories of fourth grade. To this day I can't understand how this exercise was supposed to be relevant to librarianship. Even now I can't fathom why I got only a B+. Hey, no glue showed. The other was the "slide-sync" project, a group effort. This involved devising a five minute slide show and synchronizing it with voice-over. Memories of sixth grade. The technology: circa 1962. The other chief requirement: four computer generated, computer graded multiple choice exams. See what I mean about nice work?

General reference was a pound of flesh. The teacher, a newly minted doctor of library science, rhetorically asked us if we minded being called by our first names. Mine was the lone no against a tide of yesses; she hastened to add that she expected to be called "doctor."

"After all, it was a lot of hard work."

I spent the semester chasing down two hundred mostly print reference sources and then tediously word processing an index card for each in a pedantic format. Talk about busywork! Each week there were one or two things that were next to impossible to track down. Take the much consulted *Canadian: Canada's National Bibliography.* None of the three college libraries it was convenient for me to do research in owned it. So there was nothing to do save to skulk into the redoubtable New York Public Library Center for the Humanities. And there it was in the catalog! (I lacked Internet access at home.) But when I searched for the set in the reading room, it was nowhere to be found. Time to go to the reference desk and reveal my status as a library school student to all. Who else in their senses would ever seek such an item? I waited in a long line, and when my turn came I produced the call number for the librarian. She frowned, furrowed, and hummed. She then moved wordlessly out from behind the desk. Gesturing for me to follow, she conducted me back into the reading room, along its left side. We walked up a couple of steps to the reference shelves. Between two sets of shelves was a door. She unlocked it.

"It's up there," was all she said as she pointed skyward. I thanked her and mounted a spiral staircase (creaky of course) in a dark stairwell. When I reached the top, I found that I was back in the reading room, or rather some fifteen feet above it. Here rested the kinds of things that only library students enrolled in general reference would need. Fortunately my quarry lay right in front of me. If their armor of dust was any indication, none of the volumes had left their place since the French and Indian Wars. I slipped one gingerly off, raising a choking gray tempest. I was never closer to leaving library school and returning to the teaching job from which I had taken a leave of absence. Maybe that was the point of the assignment.

I was tremendously relieved to get through that first semester. On the night of my last class I celebrated with champagne. I had put a third of my credits behind me. (I also took cataloging, which I liked.) The next semester went more smoothly, since by then I had the hang of what to do to get by. I enrolled in another reference course, on the humanities. It was also harassing but less so than the first, since the sources were generally easier to find. The one course I liked was Archives, engagingly taught by a working archivist. The syllabus was detailed and well laid out. We covered all the standard archival topics: provenance, original order, arrangement and description, preservation, and so on. Each week's class focused on what the syllabus promised. Lively discussions were routine but were never allowed to stray far from the topic. The main written assignments, which focused on arrangement and description, were challenging and directly relevant to archival work.

In the summer I took an excellent course on the history of books and printing. This was the one time that I felt as if I were back in graduate school. First, the material genuinely appealed to me. We spent the first half of the course covering tablets, manuscripts—mostly illuminated—and bindings. We devoted most of the balance to incunabula and the different styles of early printing in Germany, Italy, France, and England. The course was run like a seminar. Each week we read a sizable chunk of scholarly literature and were expected to come to class prepared to discuss it; each week the teacher put together an excellent slide show. My dilettante's interest in old books was altered into an informed appreciation by the end of the course.

I only had two courses left for fall 1997. One was on database searching, specifically LEXIS-NEXIS and DIALOG. Although I'm not convinced that one needs to take a full semester, three credit course on database searching, the librarian-teacher was excellent. She was always well prepared, and I must admit that her assignments were highly relevant to what I encountered in the trenches.

I began applying for jobs in September 1997, and by late October I had a part-time job at the busy reference desk at Pace University, a business school in lower Manhattan. I worked fifteen hours a week through the end of the semester. In January my hours were nearly doubled. Initially of course I felt overwhelmed; I kept trying to relate the questions I was facing at the desk to the four hundred reference sources that I'd been exposed to over the past thirteen months, with little success. Half the questions were for marketing assignments. Many of these were quite esoteric, e.g., how much white wine did men 35–55 in Tuscany drink year to year from 1992 through 1996? How much money has been spent in the '90s on advertising for hybrid bikes in New York and California? And so on. As the weeks passed, I felt more confident, but the increased comfort had far more to do with the hands-on than with anything I'd learned in library school.

I've now been in the field for two a half years, and I think that time has given me some perspective on the utility of library school. Part of my criticism bears specifically on the particular library school that I attended. When I started working I realized that I was being trained to work in the library of the '80s. Computers, database searching, etc., save for the one class just mentioned, were still peripheral to my training. It was possible to get one's degree with virtually no computer exposure along the way. This is the problem with having instructors who haven't worked in a library since Melvil Dewey's day.

But my main criticism of library school relates to its very existence. Library work can be interesting, challenging, and demanding. But certainly most—probably all—of the skills needed can be picked up on the job or in demonstrations and workshops. In fact some can't be learned in the classroom at all. Reference for instance isn't a classroom skill; it can really only be learned in practice. In the fourteen hours a week that I currently spend at the reference desk my proficiency at fielding questions has corresponded directly to my experience: the longer I've been at the desk, the better I've come to know the collection and the relevant databases. Any edge that my reference and database courses gave me at the outset was soon gone. And library school did nothing to prepare me for my other duties and activities: bibliographic instruction, collection development—ordering materials and weeding—and interlibrary loan. A second qualm that I have about the master's in library science is that it leads to an absurd hierarchy in libraries between "professionals" and "non-professionals." Only "professionals," i.e., those with library degrees, are allowed to work the reference desk, order books, or do bibliographic instruction, to name just three. Where I work only those with a library degree are faculty and qualify for tenure. But we all know that any reasonably intelligent person can do these jobs just as effectively without the benefit of an M.L.S. In fact the prior experience most relevant to my reference and instructional duties was my thirteen years as a teacher. I don't mean to single the MLS out for special polemic. I suspect that most of the vocational masters and doctorates that have proliferated over the last half century or so—the M.B.A., the master's in education, the Ed.D., etc.—could also disappear without academic or professional loss.

I realized many years before I actually left teaching that I wouldn't be doing it for the remainder of my working days. Teaching is extremely demanding, what with continual class prep, endless grading, and constant meetings with students. During the semester I barely had a life, and the long vacations weren't adequate compensation. Shifting my career to library work made sense in lots of ways. To begin with, I had worked in an academic library for a couple of years after I finished college. Fond memories of that time remained with me over the years. Second, I sought a field where my philosophy background might not be a liability, where there were others who had also either had or envisaged an academic career. And third, I thought that my teaching experience would be an asset with regard to bibliographic instruction.

My big break came in September 1998, when I was hired for a one semester full-time reference position at Brooklyn College. It was nice finally to be working in the library of a liberal arts school, which after all was my goal. The desk, although hectic at times, was considerably less busy than Pace. (Brooklyn College is in the middle of the borough, at the end of two subway lines; Pace is on the northern edge of Manhattan's financial district.) Most of the librarians in the reference department at Brooklyn were very experienced. All made me feel welcome, and I learned while working at the desk with them. I learned a good deal observing their different styles and trying to combine the best elements from each. I came in particular to appreciate the importance of the reference interview in pointing students in the right direction. When I wasn't at the desk, I was working in the library's excellent archives with the highly capable assistant archivist. Archival work also appealed to me; it was interesting to relate what I'd learned in class to what I was doing daily. I spent most of my time in the archives working with Brooklyn historical material. By the end of the four months I was beginning to feel like a Brooklyn native.

In November 1998 I was hired for a permanent reference position at Hunter College in Manhattan. Hunter is also a liberal arts school. And like Brooklyn College, it is part of the City University of New York. This made the transition relatively smooth, since the catalog is the same and there was almost complete overlap in the complement of databases. Moreover the position was tenure track, and this appealed to me: I was happy to accept a publishing requirement for the benefits that tenure confers. I've got excellent colleagues, and, as at Brooklyn, I was warmly received from the start. The reference desk policy of pairing less experienced librarians with the more experienced has given me the opportunity to learn a great deal in a relatively short time.

My duties at the library include selecting books and managing the collection for education, math and statistics, and physics, as well as supervising interlibrary loan. I also participate in bibliographic instruction (B.I.), doing two to three classes a week during the high season in the middle of the semester. I enjoy the challenge. I've been pleasantly surprised at the extent to which my teaching experience has prepared me for B.I. Years of getting up in front of groups day in, day out, have accustomed me to public speaking and to gauging the needs of my audience. Also, I think that the critical thinking skills that studying and teaching philosophy cultivate have helped me with B.I., with its emphasis on Boolean techniques and with assessing the authority and reliability of different sources. Although there are times when I miss the classroom, I'm glad I made the switch. I work in a solid academic library with strong book and journal collections and a healthy array of online and CD-ROM databases. (Okay, we could always use more money for both books, serials, databases, and computers, but that hardly distinguishes us from most libraries.) I've also had the opportunity to improve my computer skills significantly. First, there are the many hours that I spend at the reference desk assisting patrons with database searches. Second, I've been able to learn a great deal from my colleagues, some of whom are remarkably computer savvy. And third, I've had the time to put together my own Web page, which includes a PowerPoint presentation on Boolean searching, truncation, and proximity.

My daily routine, needless to say, is very different from what it was five years ago, when I would rush home, after an exhausting day of teaching, for an evening of several hours of class prep and paper grading. I still have busy days, but I'm happy to report that evenings are usually my own. And library school seems like a distant, slightly unpleasant, but for the most part irrelevant memory. Insofar as the experience was necessary to land a job like the one I currently have, it was worthwhile. But otherwise I remain convinced that most of the year and a half that I spent studying library science was a waste.

Libraries: A Different Perspective

David Faucheux

David Faucheux is a recent Phi Beta Kappa graduate of Louisiana State University where he also completed his M.L.I.S. and was accepted into Beta Phi Mu.

"What is a library?" Depends on whom you ask—right? For me, this question immediately conjures up that hot summer three years ago. My guide dog, Nader, and I had just entered library school at the Louisiana State University School of Library and Information Science in Baton Rouge. I had been e-mailing the dean for months endeavoring to discuss the many concerns I had. Yes, I knew I was throwing the faculty and other LSU officials a proverbial curve ball that they are still even now trying to catch. I was sitting in the auditorium, Nader blissfully half-dozing at my feet, tail occasionally twitching, wondering what I was doing here, overdressed in a silk tie and linen blazer, and listening to the dean talk about professionalism and what that meant. It may seem almost ironic to some that a blind person would even be interested in a profession that upon first consideration might seem to be so dependent on sight. For as long as I can remember, my interest in reading has been counterbalanced by the scarcity of Braille and recorded materials. From eagerly awaiting the next book in the mail during school breaks, to having my aunt look up words in her encyclopedia during long weekend visits, and later having the 145-volume 1959 edition *Braille World Book* literally at my fingertips in junior high study hall; through developing various strategies to obtain materials in high school and college, I have become increasingly concerned with the availability of print materials to the blind library patron.

"But what is a library?" you wonder. For me, that question is complicated by my rapid vision loss. I remember as a child during the endless summers of swimming lessons and crafts classes also going to the public library with my mother and brothers. They looked at shelves of books, adult novels for her, and books my mother thought we would like. She often read to us before bed. I remember wondering if breakfasting on green eggs and ham would be half as repulsive as Sam-I-am insisted and if buying a feline as sagacious as The Cat in the Hat would be possible. I remember liking the stereopticon slides that lived in a box which reposed on top of one of the low-standing bookcases in the children's room below a window. I even listened to the long-playing recordings of what I later learned were Newbery books. I just thought they were funny smelling records with a silhouette of a profile and a gold medallion. They never were long enough. I was always running out of books to hear.

"But isn't a library more?" you persist. Yes, it is. After I lost my remaining vision, I turned more and more to a different kind of library—a postal library. That's right, a postal library. Let me explain. The Library of Congress–sponsored National Library Service for the Blind and Physically Handicapped is a network of cooperating regional libraries that serve persons who meet the qualifications. I would receive mysterious black cardboard—later blue plastic—containers full of slow-playing records. My talking book machine was my magic carpet to such fantastic realms as OZ, the center of the earth, the moon, Venus, the Italy of Romeo and Juliet and the mitochondria of a cell. I endured the exquisite suspense of Madeline L'Engle, laughed at The Jack Tales and some Scott Corbett books, and was scared to death by several John Bellairs books. I had a hard and fast rule: Talking books were for home and Braille books were for school. I rarely wavered from this rule. And then four-track slow speed cassettes made their appearance. I enjoyed the portability, ease of storage, and knowing that each pale green box held hours of listening and even a kind of para-social-friendship. I even learned to speed-listen. I used the variable speed control switch to gradually increase the speed of the machine. This made reading books such as Jennings's *Aztec*, Clavell's *Noble House* or Michener's *Texas* faster by 50 percent. I do also remember the torture of waiting for the library in Baton Rouge to send a replacement for a cassette that had the impertinence to break in the machine before I had finished it.

"But aren't you leaving out something?" Well, I am. I miss the ability to browse the collection. Just feeling the books all around and taking in the feel of all that information quietly sitting there and waiting for someone to explore. I miss the feel of a well-made book, the suserration of paper pages as they whisper their secrets, I miss the heft of a thick, meaty tome full of arcane lore. I miss not being able to look at maps that jigsaw the political perplexities of the former USSR and Yugoslavia into smaller and smaller fragments. I miss not being able to examine the art books, the costume books, the books replete with elaborate drawings of technical processes and biological morphology. I miss not being able to peruse the news of yesteryear through the grainy mono-chrome reality of a microform, or handle and decode the spidery calligraphy of people who lived centuries ago. I miss not being able to visually appreciate the incunabula and other rarities of the bibliographic trade. I miss not being able to appreciate the cinematography of the geniuses of film.

"So what are you doing in the library profession?" you rightly inquire. I am here because I have a dream. I want to be heard as both a blind patron of the library and a blind librarian. I feel that this unique perspective is a rare and valuable one. This double vision should enhance any NLS regional fore-sighted enough to give me a chance. I want to contribute something to the network that has meant so much to me. I want to continue to meet the many excellent talking book narrators who have made so many books come alive for me—meet them through the books they record and meet them in person at various library functions. I want to make people aware of the rich treasure trove of recorded books archived at several talking book studios. I want to help ensure that the Internet serves as a gateway to ever-expanding sources of infor-mation.

I believe that schools and libraries always should have provided equitable services to students and patrons with visual impairments if for no other rea-son than our own professional ethics require it, most library school and library mission statements imply it, and to some extent the fiscal health of our insti-tutions depends upon it. I want to help make this happen!

You ask, "What am I doing, now?" Well, nothing! Nothing yet. I con-tinue to try to find employment or an internship that might lead to a job. I feel that I could contribute quite a lot to a library—hopefully one that chiefly serves blind and physically impaired patrons—as I have the credential, and being blind I can offer unique insights into both what it is like as a patron and what the librarian might do to help blind patrons become more information literate. I wish Nader were here with me on my continuing journey but he is not. Nader died midway through my time at grad school on February 23, 1998, as a result of a hemangio-sarcoma of the heart, lungs, and liver. Dogs are vic-tims of cancer, too. I continue in my efforts to find a job and to write letters to the administration at LSU to encourage them to make changes so that any future blind person who wishes to attend the library school there will have up-to-date access to electronic reserves and other material in the main library, a sympathetic support staff, and an atmosphere of advocacy and … I dream on. Dreams do not die, and I hope Nader knows that I made it.

Too Short to Shelve Books

Jocelyn Berger

Jocelyn Berger is an instructor at the Brooklyn College Library where she is the social sciences librarian in the reference division.

Having received my library science degree only four years ago, I probably should not be as surprised as I am by the way the computer industry has managed to alter the structure and function of libraries. Still, I am. Brooklyn College Library, like most libraries at institutions of higher learning where I've worked since graduation, has changed immensely in that short time. Part of the change is due to the fact that our building is undergoing renovation. A new wing is being added and, when it is completed some time in the year 2001, it will be remarkable. Until then my cubicle has been moved into a prefabricated building near the college's athletic field, aptly named the Field Library. Located at the far end of campus, convenient is not exactly the word I would use. Many of my colleagues, who work in other library units, are dispersed to different buildings on campus. There are a total of three campus locations. Students and faculty usually have an intellectually stimulating experience merely finding the library. The second reason for the difference is technology. Much as the typewriter revolutionized the profession by eliminating the need to write catalog cards by hand, advances in technology continue to determine the skills we need to serve our patrons.

I chose this profession, or rather this profession chose me, because I love books. What is more important, I love information. I love that I can answer questions. When my mother wants the names of Sidney Lumet's films to solve a word puzzle, she knows that within a minute she will have a list complete with the release dates. The same is true for most questions she comes up with. Each time I present her with the requested information—country capitals, the names of popes, from my home library, no less—she gives me the same look of amazement. Had I turned lead into gold, I expect I would get much the same look. This is not an uncommon reaction.

It is that look that convinced me to become a librarian.

My desire to do this for a living has always seemed self-serving. I perceived it as showing off the way children do when they've learned to count to ten or to recite their ABCs. I had a special talent. I felt exceptional. Imagine my surprise when my family and friends, the people who knew me better than anyone else, questioned my decision. They believed that I was settling for a boring job. Only boring people became librarians.

Librarians are stereotyped as anal-retentive, compulsive organizers (a quick glance at my apartment belies that statement), boring, prudish, socially awkward, and possessing no sense of humor. Donna Reed's 1946 portrayal of a librarian in *It's a Wonderful Life* is still with us. While I knew this characterization could not be true, still it worried me. I foresaw going to parties or meeting people for the first time and being asked the inevitable question "So what do you do?" I never envisioned the response being anything remotely like, "You're a librarian. That must be so exciting!" I was right. This hardly ever happens, no matter how enthusiastically I state my profession.

The usual response is "Oh," followed by an awkward moment of silence as they consider what to say next. This is often preferable to some longer responses I have received. Once I was told that I seemed too short to shelve books for a living. What I've come to realize is that most people do not know what librarians do. Still, I applied to library school and joined the ranks of the misunderstood.

In library school I learned my craft and its history. I learned about reference work, the reference interview, cataloging, the history of books and libraries, the repair, care, and proper storage and handling of books, budgeting, management, and lastly, minimally, computers. There was one required course on the basics of computers and their applications in the library, a course which did not discuss the Internet except in the most abstract terms. The professor of my reference course discussed the pros and cons of Internet-based databases and journals. In the access-ownership debate—on whether access to databases or journals was preferable to owning (and having to store) the same materials—she was clearly on the ownership side of the argument. She distrusted the model wherein one has access to a resource only as long as one subscribes. No matter how high the quality of an Internet resource, it lacks tangibility and permanence. It serves people in the present, but can disappear at any time. It goes against the instinct of many of us who preserve knowledge for the future, which is another reason the profession appealed to me. Some people call me a pack rat, but the thought of bringing together and preserving books and journals that will serve library patrons long after I've left the library stirs something in me. It's as if I were leaving the world, or a small corner of it, better than when I found it. I foresee the joy of looking back someday, having helped create something of use.

Still, the Internet called to me. In 1995, I logged on from home for the first time. I was forever changed.

Each night, from ten P.M. to the early hours of the morning, I found out what this new information tool was all about. The amount of information available on the Internet seemed immense. I explored the trivial and the scholarly. I found free printable, downloadable versions of writings (beyond the restrictions of copyright); the *New York Times* online; up-to-date episode guides on fan-operated Web sites for my favorite television programs; and databases on every conceivable subject. I found a lot of shopping. I also found a lot of misinformation, pornography, and personal home pages where people had uploaded pictures of their pets and children. There is a good deal of this and with most ISPs (Internet Service Providers) offering free Web pages to their customers, these pages will only increase. The web is a mixed bag of the superlative, the mediocre and the downright awful.

Now, in the year 2000, there is practically no limit to what one can buy or learn on the Internet. For a fee, a great selection of in-print books are downloadable to one's hard drive. Baen Publishing offers "WebScriptions," entire books or chapters of upcoming books that are available at a price, online, before the print copies appear in bookstores. The majority of the print databases and indexes I used, both in library school and my undergraduate research, are now available, for a great deal of money, in Web-based versions. That number will increase.

Internet technology is constantly changing, and I know I have to keep up. I suppose it is fortunate that, even now, the Internet still fascinates me. Its potential is awesome. What ultimately upgrades or replaces it will be more so. In the not too distant future, computers should have the capacity to respond reliably to voice commands and typing may become obsolete. I cannot wait to see what comes next.

And of course I am not alone in this obsession. The nation as a whole and the members of my profession especially have become aspiring technogeeks. We seek to master the secrets of computers, and this is likely related to our instinct to survive. No longer is it sufficient to be a good librarian. Each type of library requires different minimum computer skills. Most require at least basic mastery of word processing and Internet use, and many will require or reward more advanced knowledge. For this and other reasons, library journals are currently replete with articles on the Internet. Several recurring topics are: how to instruct people in using the Internet, how to search the Internet effectively, how to design Web pages for libraries, how to select Web-based products, how to design and read online catalogs, and how copyright law affects the Internet.

I thought for a time that the Internet would make my job obsolete. If I could find a lot of the information I wanted without leaving my bedroom, I suspected that others could do the same. Of what use, then, would libraries, with their limited hours, be? Of what use librarians? I suspected that I would see, in my lifetime, the end of the profession, save for the one librarian remaining at each library, who would sit overlooking a large bank of computer terminals. And even that much contact might not be necessary.

One future option might be to place a phone by each terminal, like the ones we now have in ATMs, which allow customers to contact bank personnel if assistance is required. The phone would be used in conjunction with software that would give the librarian a view of the patron's screen. This would eliminate the need for the librarian to be in the same room with the person being helped. Another version of this idea would involve the use of video technology, some of which already exists. Live action images (and sound) of the librarian helping the patron would appear in a corner of the computer screen, while images (and sound) of the patron would be simultaneously transmitted to the librarian. But neither, I expect, will occur any time soon.

While books will still circulate, I believe that for reference service, in less than one generation, this computer-based library will be the norm. I am not certain how I feel about this just yet. When I work at the reference desk, I conduct a reference interview to get a firm grasp of what the patron is seeking, and my first thought is whether a print book exists in our collection that would provide the information requested. Often, the answer is "no." Next, I mentally run through the sizable list of databases to determine which one(s) will work best in that particular instance. The student will often require a brief introduction to the particular database. Over time, I suspect, the student body, having been brought up using computers in their homes and schools, will be far more savvy about figuring these things out for themselves. So of how much use will I be in the years to come?

This is the academic library of the future as I see it. It is not the library I went to library school to prepare for. I can see the changes already. A recent example of this is our library's new Web page. I have been involved in designing it, and the process has been long, each decision made very deliberately. We want our Web page to be professional, functional, and inviting and we are working hard to make it so. Many of the library's research tools, including our catalog, can be searched using the Web page as a gateway. Perhaps that Web page may be all certain people ever "see" of the library. If they are using it off-campus, from home, work, or from a Kinko's, no librarian will be available to help them. Therefore, we hope it will be easy to use.

However, the thought of this makes me uneasy. I will never see these people at the reference desk. I will never hear them call to see if we have a book. I will not know if they are finding the information they are seeking, or if they are failing to locate items the library owns because they don't know how to search the online catalog. Worse, yet, I won't even know if they exist. In the digital age, I won't know who, if anyone, I am helping.

And Brooklyn College is a commuter school. Many of our students take classes while working full-time. Many have families and other responsibilities. These students will naturally seek to work in the most time-efficient way possible. Anything that eliminates time spent traveling to campus is a big help to these students, even it means having fewer research options. If the public library is closer, they will go there instead.

Recently, the library began offering access to two superlative Web-based databases, American History and Life, and Historical Abstracts. They are currently available on a trial basis, but will undoubtedly be purchased. When I was teaching a group of graduate students in history, I mentioned these new offerings and the response was good. But when a student asked if the databases could be accessed from home, and I said no, everyone stopped copying the URL (uniform resource locator). Their interest in these resources died as soon as they learned that they had to be on a CUNY campus, any one of nineteen campuses in New York City, to use them.

So who am I building a collection for? Why am I buying books, as they, too, require the patron to come to the library to read or borrow them? With the growing availability of online books, will borrowing books also become a "remote" function of the library? In years to come, just how many books will be available online? Students will only have to type in the title and author to find a book and save it to their home computers or if they are actually at the library, to save it to the zip drives connected to the terminals here. The zip disk can then be used with their home computers. The only books that will be out-of-print will be those that the publisher chooses to make unavailable for reasons of copyright or age and currency of the material. Economics, the cost of printing and storing the physical books, will matter far less. If publishers pursue this avenue of book distribution, it will change my work considerably. After all, why buy a copy of a book that may sit on a shelf unread when students can request books as the need arises?

While this is a logical way of providing books for our students and faculty, it will rob me of one of my greatest pleasures. The first time I saw a newly arrived book that I had ordered on a shelving cart, I felt as if I had really done something noteworthy. A book was in the library because I had decided that it should be there. I felt powerful. Buying access to a collection of electronic books is not likely to produce that emotion.

But electronic book usage is not as likely to happen as quickly as other practices will. The speed will be determined by the actions of the publishing houses, advances in technology, and possibly most important, the funding that schools and university libraries receive for accessing such expensive online resources. If the money is not available, or allocated elsewhere, which I expect will be the case, then the tangible books I grew up with will remain on library shelves for quite some time.

The expectations of our patrons, a growing number of them anyway, have clearly been keeping pace with the technology. Many of our students and faculty know what is available on the Internet and want all of it. They believe the hype that everything is available on the Internet, free and easy to find. Some resent having to make copies of journal articles when they should be online and printable. The idea seems to be that the change in format, from print to electronic, should reduce the time needed to research any topic to under an hour.

These students almost always think it is quicker to search the Internet for information, even when sitting in the library less than twenty feet away from the reference collection. Even then, many log on to read a copy of the Declaration of Independence. And they will find it online, at many different Web sites. It will probably take longer to find online than if they had looked in any of the several encyclopedias on our shelves, but that will likely never occur to them. Asking the librarian at the reference desk will likely not occur to them either until they have spent an unsuccessful half hour looking on their own.

In all fairness, I should point out that my library, like any other library, has problems that make the Internet the preferred option. Books with pages that have been torn out, broken photocopy machines and change machines are chief among these. So the students are not always wrong in turning to the Internet as a source for material found in printed form. But my concern is that I will never know whether I could have helped them when they are stuck.

In our original library building, I could make myself accessible. The Internet terminals were a few steps away from the reference desk. Since they were arranged in a circular pattern, I could walk around them as if checking the machines, letting them know that help was available, while glancing at monitors to see if students were actually getting what they wanted. But now that we have moved to a temporary prefabricated building, the computers are placed in rows facing a wall. I can no longer gauge discreetly who may need help. The Internet stations are not much further away from me than they had been, but the slight alteration in furniture placement creates a blind spot. I'm certain that I now seem as far away as the moon to some users. And some will be too shy to seek me out.

I have noticed that while I am interacting with fewer people at the reference desk, I do spend, on average, more time, with each person I do help. To get patrons started on a database, to the point where they can work on their own, usually requires more time than it did to show them how to use a print index or the current library catalog. More time is spent with patrons at the opposite end of the computer-literacy spectrum, the people who rarely, if ever, use computers for anything other than word processing and are hesitant to go online. I find this role comforting. I reassure people that nothing they do will damage the computer, that no one is born knowing how to use one, that everyone must have their turn at learning. Thus I usher them into the computer world (and facilitate my own obsolescence).

A big problem that our reliance on computers creates is that, at the most inconvenient times, we lose our connection. This can happen for any number of reasons, and there is very little that librarians can do to provide access. Right now we can still access the library catalog, which allows the student to locate both reference and circulating books. But recently it has been decided that the library catalog will be changing over to a Web-based system. While its capabilities will increase a great deal, the effect is that this resource too will cease to be available when the Internet connection is lost. It is difficult to describe the frustration I feel when I have to tell patrons that I can't help them because "the Web is down." To say that they get discouraged would be an understatement. People are justifiably put off.

So, we still have some kinks to work out. And with the pace of technology's advance, I doubt we will ever catch up. I do not think we were meant to. Maybe understanding this is the key to maintaining one's sense of commitment and sanity. I only hope that as the library changes, there continues to be a place for librarians and a place for books. In any case, I am determined to see what happens next. It may be a bumpy ride, but it is one I don't want to miss.

The President and
the Revolutionary

Bruce Jensen

Bruce Jensen is a student in the Graduate School of Education and Information Studies at UCLA. He still calls it library school, and is pursuing a joint master's degree in Latin American Studies. He is a founding member of the Activist Librarians and Educators.

At a recent librarians' conference—one of those edifying gatherings where scores of sour-faced people sleep late, sneak out for sightseeing, and collect receipts for use on tax returns and per diem vouchers—I listened to plenary addresses delivered by the presidents of two prominent professional organizations.

Asked to predict what issues would be important in libraries ten years hence, one of these leaders pierced straight to the core of the question. Never mind such trivia as intellectual freedom, equity of access, or the role of technology. No, a lot of wild ideas have been advanced, she told us, but in her opinion the one goal worth shooting for was the idea that ten years from now the highest-salaried member of any corporation could be its information manager.

That, she told us, was really something to strive for.

Well, arguably what elevates one to the executive suite of a large national organization is not idealism, nor the knack of giving substantial answers to serious questions. Perhaps more potent insights were to be expected from her counterpart at the head of a much larger librarians' club.

This chief related an anecdote about a young man, a brown-skinned foreigner who had wandered into her neighborhood to do menial labor of some sort. She ended up giving the unfortunate stranger in a strange land a ride back out to civilization, and was "absolutely astonished" to learn that he had a number of kinfolk in town. The adventure, happily, turned out to be mutually rewarding.

"When I dropped him off," the eminent librarian said, "I gave him money, and of course he loved me."

But of course, agreed the charmed chuckles from the audience. The story continued. "That same day, I asked my dry cleaner of ten years where she came from. And would you believe, it was the same part of Mexico that boy was from!" As the room buzzed at this anecdotal confirmation of the well-documented social phenomenon called chain migration, I had a question of my own: Who gives her dirty clothes to someone for ten years without once asking the woman where she's *from*?

My mind drifted to thoughts of how a library group's president might be removed from office. Had one ever been impeached? Maybe I could allege sexual impropriety by taking out of context the phrase, "I gave him money ... *and he loved me.*"

But I could feel the audience's support for this confident dynamo at the lectern. Now it was I who was drifting in the wrong neighborhood. What jolted me back to consciousness was hearing an obvious fallacy: "Mexican immigrants can't know much about libraries," our speaker said, "because after all the public library has *only a ten- or twelve-year history*" in their benighted homeland.

This was news to me. My own memories of using public libraries in Mexico prior to that time, were they dreams? I pinched myself; was not dreaming. I remembered reading about a public library founded in Mexico in 1826, knew I was fascinated by the life of José Vasconcelos, the Secretary of Education credited with founding thousands of libraries throughout the country in the 1920s, and I even recalled attending this same library conference in a Mexican city whose central public library was at the time celebrating its silver anniversary.

After the president's speech I talked to other attendees to gauge their level of cognitive dissonance. There were after all some genuine Mexican librarians in the crowd.

Library history, I discovered, might be made by selfless heroes, and written by noble scribes, but it is liable to be erased and rewritten by the leaders of influential professional organizations. Everyone I spoke with was honored by the president's presence, and certainly pleased with what she told us. Yes, the public library—such a new and baffling concept for those Mexicans.

I have here a Spanish-language volume called *Vasconcelos: The Man of the Book*—or as Lawrence Clark Powell would have doubtless preferred to translate the phrase, "Bookman." It would be a shame to ignore the work of this scholar, politician, and activist, Vasconcelos. Whatever his faults, he expressed and acted upon a fervent passion for books, holding an innocent conviction about their power to rescue and redeem humanity.

Vasconcelos was one of those for whom books are medicine, magic, music, and manna. The salvation he found in libraries during an itinerant youth in Mexico and the U.S. was a gift he sought to share with his fellow citizens, and he had the guts to jump on a horse and join the rebels—this was the era of Pancho Villa, remember—in order to do that. Vasconcelos operated as an agent in Washington, D.C., on behalf of the Mexican revolutionaries.

After he helped topple an entrenched, intensely classist regime, Vasconcelos was appointed Mexico's Secretary of Education. Armed with a budget that multiplied pre–Revolution spending, he attacked his task as a warrior for pedagogy, driven by what folks in those days used to call the "library spirit." You have heard of this, perhaps. It is the impulse, perhaps naïve but astonishingly powerful, to go door-to-door begging books, then load them on the back of a mule, trudging through mud and sand toward someone who might want to read them.

Vasconcelos worked stalwartly to set up public libraries, workers' libraries, mobile libraries, school libraries, determined to bring the gift of the book to the deepest hidden corners of the republic—a republic he had risked his own well-being to help establish. After a time he even campaigned for its presidency, but learned the hard way that politics has little room for the sorts of people who are infected with ideals like his. Exiled for many years, he finally returned to Mexico to serve in a position less celebrated but more noble than the presidency: Director of the National Library.

You might well imagine that in present-day Mexico, where government funds tend to wander off before being distributed locally, it takes a hell of a lot of that old library spirit to keep the doors open and the books on the shelves. There I have seen many backroom volunteer repair workshops, where clamps and white glue are applied to beat-up volumes that U.S. librarians would have dumped long ago. I have watched children's programs, delightful story sessions, built around props made from cardboard boxes, broom handles, and hours of careful preparation. And I have been in library buildings with no running water where electricity comes in from next door by means of extension cords.

Many librarians here in Southern California and other parts of the U.S. have "informed" me that lending libraries do not exist in Mexico, that these immigrants therefore have no concept of what a library is, that all they want are comic books, and that anyway most of them can't read.

Working in a library in the same searing Sonoran desert where Vasconcelos himself spent much of his childhood, I used to check books out using a rubber date stamp instead of a laser bar code scanner. But those books came back on time and people seemed to appreciate the chance to take them home. They knew how to read, as far as I could tell; even seemed to enjoy it.

The library's classroom, where I taught the odd course, had a warped blackboard that pulled away from the wall and catapulted chalk chunks out into the peanut gallery if I wasn't careful how I wrote. That library had old books and gray walls and an unreliable cooling system. It had dogs, too, because the librarian was a poodle-lover, and a black-and-white television at the circulation desk because he was a baseball fan.

It is tempting to list the apparent handicaps that Mexican librarians must cope with and overcome in order to create dynamic, inspiring centers of learning and community. The list is long, and the solutions have often been brilliant. But do not misunderstand—I am not calling for spoiled-rotten U.S. librarians to stop complaining and learn to make do with less. Austerity measures are too often rewarded with administrative pats on the back and deeper budget cuts; artful complaining has a crucial function in serving our communities.

Nor do I intend to shake the scolding forefinger and urge colleagues to catch the library spirit. That is something you either have or you don't—but with an open mind you are bound to catch it in time. That spirit is not, by the way, something they give you in library school, though they might do their best to take it away from you. Jose Vasconcelos, it bears mentioning here, did not hold any M.L.I.S. degree.

No, the lesson for us in the president's speech is to be careful about diminishing the work and the knowledge of our forebears, here and abroad. To avoid misjudging, and hence mis-serving, our patrons. We owe it to them to respect their knowledge and their history.

Once a co-worker, a reference librarian at a public library, complained that the local high school students were overrunning her desk for requests for books about revolutions. Their assignment was to write about any revolution they chose.

"That sounds interesting," I said.

"Well, there's just not that much material. I mean, after the American, French, and Russian revolutions, what else is there, really?"

I mentioned Nicaragua, Cuba, El Salvador. "And how 'bout the Mexican Revolution? That must be pretty interesting, don't you think?"

"Oh," she replied, "those revolutions don't really *count.*"

How would Vasconcelos, the revolutionary, the librarian, have felt had he heard such a dismissal? And from a *colleague*—if that is even an apt word for her. How can we claim to be peers of a fighter spirited enough to change his faulty government in order to advance the cause of learning and libraries, if we don't even bother to change our own faulty thinking?

We U.S. librarians may no longer need the force of the library spirit in order to light our buildings or even build an acquisitions budget. But we still have a responsibility to our communities, to understand who they are and how we can work on their behalf. There's no longer any need to trudge through the mud beside a mule in order to get library work done, yet there remains—and always will—the messy work of trudging the sidewalks of the library's neighborhood, getting to know people. Not giving them books or videos or money and expecting them to, of course, love us: just getting to *know* them. If we give that a chance, we might find it at least as rewarding and instructive as anything we'll hear at a professional conference.

The Recruitment of a Librarian: A Personal Memoir

Lina M. Lowry

Lina M. Lowry has retired from the Borough of Manhattan Community College of the City University of New York where she served as chief librarian. Currently, she volunteers as congregational librarian at the Trinity Church of New York where she is cataloging at last.

My family moved to Philadelphia from a small town in Virginia when I was three years old. When I was six my father's company moved him again—to Pittsburgh. Six years later the company moved him back to Philadelphia. Each move was exciting to me and traumatic for my mother. I always liked helping to pack up the books again and didn't mind at all that I wasn't allowed to touch the dishes and other more fragile possessions.

More than just the chore of moving though, my mother feared urban neighborhoods. She had been born into a well-to-do Negro (notice the capital "N") family. She was put off by the low class of our neighbors. This makes her sound snobbish but it was more than that. In Virginia you knew who your neighbors were. They had probably lived in the same house for a generation. In Pittsburgh this was a real problem because I was then old enough to go about on my own (a little bit—to school, to the store). Whenever she asked me about the family of some school friend she would be appalled that I did not know what the father did for a living or exactly where the family hailed from. While she did not mind my bringing some friend to sit on our steps, she would not allow me to go into anyone else's house unless she at least had met the mother. I was expected to be visible and in calling distance at all times.

In both Philadelphia and Pittsburgh she was able to locate an Episcopal church with a Negro congregation where she became active and involved me in Sunday School and the Girls Friendly Society. She had been a YWCA secretary in her hometown so she affiliated with that organization too. And I got to attend dance classes, Y-teen activities, and summer camp. We had brought a melodeon from Virginia which barely survived our move to Pittsburgh where my father got a good deal on a secondhand upright piano. So when I was five my mother found a music teacher in the neighborhood and started me on music lessons. She persisted in this folly until I was in junior high school. I had a very structured childhood, which I felt was extremely boring.

Pittsburgh in those days was very sooty. It was war time and the steel mills caused the night skies to glow pink. I developed asthma. It seemed to me that I spent a lot of time in bed trying to breathe the benzoin fumes from the brew on the stove. Polio was a frightening disease and my mother had learned that it came from public pools so there was no possibility that I would learn how to swim in those hot summers. The hills and the streetcar tracks made bicycling look dangerous so my tricycle was never replaced with a two-wheeler. I think I learned to roller skate while we were in Philly the first time. In Pittsburgh we lived on one street that was cobbled (not good for skating). One Christmas I received a pair of skating shoes so I could go on Saturdays to the Kay Boys Club or the YMCA, which both had rinks.

Looking back on those days, boring as they were, under my mother's controlling thumb, I think the best thing that happened to me was when on one of our first walks through the fearsome Hill District we discovered the Wylie Avenue Branch of the Carnegie Library of Pittsburgh. This was a new institution for my mother. In Virginia there were no public libraries for colored people. My mother immediately signed up for a library card and signed for me to get one too.

For as long as we remained in Pittsburgh, I was always allowed to go to the library by myself. At our branch I read my way around the children's room. I remember reading every color of Andrew Lang's fairy tales. There was a great collection of books about American Indians (as they were called in those days) illustrated with the most wonderful photography. I became something of an authority on various tribes. As I grew older I was even allowed to take the streetcar over into Oakland to the main library where the children's collection was huge. Titles like *For Cross and Crown*, *The Lost Queen of Egypt*, and *The Cloister and the Hearth* stay in my memory. I read everything illustrated by Howard Pyle and N.C. Wyeth. I discovered Percival Christopher Wren and Rafael Sabatini and Alexandre Dumas and even adult authors like Thomas Costain and Samuel Shellabarger.

Another thing that is vivid in my recollection is that in A. Leo Weil Elementary School on Centre Avenue in Pittsburgh our classes had regular library periods in which Mrs. Swingle would read us stories. She never finished them and the only way I could find out how a book ended was by borrowing the book and finishing it myself. My father knew a man who owned a book store in the Hill District and he would let me go with him to browse. I still have *Word Pictures of Great Negroes* that he bought for me on one of our visits. I think it was through that association that we were introduced to the Sunday *New York Times* which we ever after were addicted to for its magazine, book reviews, and advertisements of plays and movies. (One of the first places I wanted to see when I finally visited New York was Marboro Books.)

I had already finished one term at Herron Hill Junior High School when my father's job moved him back to Philadelphia. There my mother and I discovered the Kingsessing Branch of the Free Library of Philadelphia, which was on the way walking to the Anna Howard Shaw Junior High School. Even though I had school tickets to ride the trolley, I often elected to walk so I could go to the library on the way home.

I had a multi-volume set of my own books. It was red with black labels. It had fairy tales, myths and legends, nature study, and some others I don't remember. Sometimes I would stack up the volumes to improvise doll furniture. We also had a multiple volume set of history books with pictures, which I loved. I think that is why I always loved historical novels and movies with flashing swords and long dresses, and men in tights. I regret to say that these important artifacts of my childhood are all lost now. I suspect that my mother may have left them behind even though I had lovingly packed them.

When I began college at Temple University, freshmen were given a walking tour of the largely concrete campus including the magnificent Sullivan Library. I believe that was all the bibliographic instruction I ever received there but, because libraries had become my home away from home, I felt equal to the task of decoding this one. Here I encountered the Library of Congress (LC) classification for the first time. It was very mysterious. The Sullivan Library had closed stacks. The only way I could get the feel of this complex system was by roaming in its excellent reference collection, which had open shelves. There was also a small, comfortable browsing room presided over by a tall, white-haired woman who was very helpful and much friendlier than she looked.

I was a junior when I got a job as a student aide in the circulation department of the library, running up the eight floors of stacks with call slips to retrieve titles requested by other students. Little did I realize then what a turning point this was to be in my life. It was so exciting to be able to actually see the collection. As LC became clearer to me, I would often bring the student substitute titles when the ones indicated on the call slips were unavailable. I earned fifty cents an hour and stack privileges and became acquainted with all the staff. I also met the man I would marry, a graduate student who used one of the carrels on level D, E, and F. I began to formulate a real plan for my future.

I had entered the College of Liberal Arts and Sciences as a premed student. This ambition foundered in the laboratories of Chemistry I and II where I learned to really appreciate a passing "D" while realizing that science did not appear to be my forte. Some fine print in the college catalog informed me that there were several courses in the education curriculum which would allow me to apply for a provisional teaching certificate in Pennsylvania upon graduation. Although teaching was not high on my list of possible careers, it seemed prudent to be prepared to do something profitable at the end of four years. So I dutifully fitted Educational Psychology, Human Geography, and (a course I remember as) Introduction to Children into my liberal arts distribution. I selected history as my major and English as a minor. My path in these disciplines was eased by the stack privileges which accrued to my lowly student aide position. Working in close association with librarians helped me to visualize a career path suitable to my interests. I learned that the Sullivan Library had a position for a paraprofessional, which, by custom, was allotted to someone who was going to library school. They recommended that I apply to the GSLS at Drexel Institute of Technology (now Drexel University). I was accepted as a part-time student at Drexel and upon graduation from Temple I was hired to work in the Cataloging Division. I think I received the grand sum of $128 a month and the privilege of being able to adjust my 40 hours so that I could attend an evening class each week.

I loved the job. I'd get miles of multiple copy book orders, file them, order LC cards, file the temporary card in the public catalog. When the actual books came upstairs from Acquisitions, I accessioned them using a Bates numbering machine, matched them with the cards that had already arrived or assigned them to the appropriate cataloger's shelves based on their subject. When cataloging was completed, books were sent upstairs to the bindery for labeling. I had a color-coded filing system so that each month I could send inquiries about non-received titles to Acquisitions. When books came from the bindery, I checked to see that the labels were correct and sent the last part of the order form to the faculty member or academic department that had ordered it. Each day I spent an hour filing cards, letter by letter, into the public catalog. What I learned on the job was helpful to me in my library school classes. I took all the cataloging courses that were offered and dreamed of becoming a cataloger.

In 1960, at the end of three years, I completed my course of study and accepted a public service position in the Brooklyn Public Library (BPL). It had only one position for a professional cataloger which was already occupied by someone who was young, hale, and hardy. But I also had a dream of living in New York. And then began the exciting and sometimes bewildering job of learning to be a librarian. The BPL was a marvelous training ground. I was mentored by experienced librarians. Working as an adult services specialist at disparate branches, I stayed at BPL for ten years, at which point a colleague told me about a job she had interviewed for at the Borough of Manhattan Community College (BMCC) of the City University of New York. She had decided to take a job at the American Library Association. So I sent a résumé and was interviewed. I was offered the position of periodicals librarian. I took it and begin a rewarding 25 years occupying every possible position except cataloger. I acquired a second master's so that I could climb the academic ladder, discovered a talent for administration, rose or fell (master of all, ergo, servant of all) to the position of chief librarian from which I retired in 1995. Now I am an adjunct librarian one evening each week at the reference desk at BMCC and volunteer in the resource center (where I actually get to catalog) of my parish. My new dream is to become as comfortable using the Internet for reference as I have always felt with book collections.

If this rambling autobiographical essay has a point or a moral it is that good librarians are the best advertisement there is for the library profession. At various retirement festivities, I was pleased to be greeted by several young people who have become librarians who were kind enough to say that I had encouraged them. We should always take time with student aides, hourly workers, summer interns, clients at the reference desk, to impart to them our love for what we do, and make it possible for them to experience or examine the different tasks that, taken together, are part of the seamless operation that good libraries present to their users. We should emphasize that no job in a library is unimportant, that each contributes to the success of the whole, that each can be a step on the ladder to positions that carry more prestige and more responsibility.

Why Weatherly (and Small Towns Like It) Should Have a Library

Ruth Isenberg

Ruth Isenberg is editor-in-chief of Journal Newspapers, *five community publications in northeastern Pennsylvania, which she operates with her husband, Seth.*

Weatherly Borough needed a library. The community of about 4,000 in northeastern Pennsylvania had actually needed a library for some time and had unsuccessfully tried to organize one about 50 years ago. We decided it was time for another try.

I had grown up nearby and visited my grandmother in her home in the community when I was a child. I remember being taken to the high school library during the summer to borrow books, but that option was no longer open to the community in 1993 when my husband and I moved into her then-vacant house.

Once we got settled, I went out to look for my closest library. I tried nearby Hazleton. Because it was in another county, it had a fee of $10, certainly not an outrageous amount to someone who supports libraries in general and the library she uses in particular. However, I was taken aback to learn that my $10 would not get me statewide borrowing privileges through PA Access. Assuming that the problem was one of crossing county lines, I next tried Jim Thorpe. Different library, same story. Since Carbon County doesn't have a county library system, and since my community didn't support one of the existing libraries, I was welcome to have a card, but I couldn't have statewide loan access. This made me mad. Having lived in a number of places with excellent library services, and having visited small towns in my husband's native New England, each with its own community library center, I didn't like seeing libraries undervalued.

I'm fortunate that my line of work as a newspaper editor gives me an outlet to express my feelings. I have to admit that most of my editorials go unremarked. Sometimes I make someone angry enough to respond with a letter, or more typically, an anonymous phone call. Occasionally, someone tells me they agree with me. People do not generally jump to follow my advice. I was quite surprised, therefore, when I got six phone calls in response to my editorial that argued that Weatherly needed a library. Not only did six individuals call, they all promised to come to a meeting to discuss the idea.

Actually, 12 people showed up for the meeting, mostly women in their thirties and forties, with one borough official and one school administrator, two husbands (one of whom was the borough official) and one high school librarian. She was there mainly to discourage us from trying to create a public library in conjunction with the school library. She did a good job. Once we got started, we decided she was probably right.

Discouragement was something we heard quite a lot of. We invited the district librarian to speak to our group, which was steadily growing. She did ... and she spent the first halfhour telling us how impractical it was for us to consider starting a traditional library with a reference department and all the trappings. However, as we continued to ask questions and come up with suggestions, she warmed to our group and ended up by giving us some good, practical advice.

Good practical advice and assistance from librarians was another commodity which was not in short supply. We were amazed at the number of librarians we actually knew, or almost knew: daughters of fellow church members, neighbors, former neighbors, in-laws, retired professionals who read newspaper articles about our efforts. The publicity began when we let the public know we were accepting donations of used books. At first, we just wanted to sell used books to raise some seed money. We asked. We were overwhelmed with contributions, many of them fairly new and in excellent condition.

As part of a community event, we held our first book sale and made a few hundred dollars. But we had hundreds of books left over, stored in our garages and living rooms. We needed a spot to begin. The local Presbyterian Church, an older congregation without a Sunday School, offered use of their social hall. We moved in, and boxes of books were everywhere. While we appreciated the church's hospitality, we knew it wasn't a good permanent location. So as we sorted through books, we searched for a home.

We tried all kinds of places, and talked to everyone we could think of. One of our appeals was to a local bank branch. The bank owned a commercial property that was attached to the building that housed the branch. There were apartments upstairs, and there had been a general store downstairs, complete with a soda fountain. It had gone out of business earlier that year, and no buyers had come forth. One day, out of the blue, we got a telephone call from the branch manager telling us that the contract was ready for our signature. What contract? The contract to lease us the storefront, at no charge, on a month-by-month basis. Our group, when it got together that week, was stunned, amazed, excited, and immensely grateful. We lost no time in signing.

Volunteers made the space ready. Cleaning was a major chore. Years of cigarette smoke had yellowed the walls and ceiling. We scrubbed, we dusted, we scrubbed some more. We found some very strange things hidden behind radiators and inside cupboards. Painting crews spruced up all the accessible surfaces with paint donated by the local hardware store. A professional painter volunteered his services to finish the upper walls and ceilings. Our shelves came from the old high school building. Its fixtures had been sold at auction. The construction company owner who had purchased them donated them to us outright. Another local contractor built children's shelves with donated materials. Even the plumbing work and fixtures were donated, and the electrician only charged for supplies.

It took about two months to ready the space. We held a community book chain to pass some of the books the two blocks from the church to the new library, one person to the next. This event was primarily symbolic, most of the boxes were moved earlier by pick-up truck, but assembling over a hundred townspeople to form a chain to hand books one after the other down the street was a spirit builder and a great photo-op. (We moved just in time for the church, which was coming into its supper and bazaar season.)

It was then that we realized what an overwhelming job we still had ahead of us. Here we were, in what seemed like a huge space, with boxes and boxes of books which had to be organized into a real library. We sat down with our Dewey decimal books, and got to work. We had some help from professionals at this point. One retired librarian spent several days helping us sort and sift. A school librarian and good friend from Massachusetts who was on medical leave from her job took a week to visit. She spent most of her time at the library, and when she left, we had a good handle on cataloging, organizing, and most importantly weeding. Meanwhile, we continued to receive donations of books. With our new knowledge of weeding, we started to be a bit more selective, gently turning down *Reader's Digest Condensed Books*, and encyclopedia sets from the sixties. We even discarded some musty, mildewed volumes and that was a very hard thing for many of us to do.

It was going to take a major effort to get all the books processed. So we called for short-term intensive aid from the community, and we got it. During May and June, we had daily work parties. Ten to 12 volunteers worked each day on cataloging. We set a goal for our grand opening, the end of July. Our grand opening celebration was fun, it attracted a great many people, including some who haven't been back since. But that is part of what a community library is, I believe, a service people want to know is available, even if they themselves don't care to use it.

The people who became involved in preparing the library were not always the same as those who maintained it. A core group regards the library as our primary cause outside of our families and our jobs. For the most part, our reasons are selfish. We enjoy reading, we have gained immeasurably from books and the knowledge that books make available to us, and we think that it's important that other people have the same opportunity. People with young children were especially active in setting the library up, because they wanted a place where reading was valued for their children. One woman noted that she felt it was important her children get to see people outside of the family, adults as well as other children, who valued books and reading. Indeed, some strong friendships have formed on this basis among people who otherwise might not have gotten to know each other well. Parents who attended storytimes with their children talked while their children listened, and found they had things in common.

The same thing has happened when we have conducted adult activities. A local insurance agent leads a music appreciation group. His seminars have attracted people of various ages and backgrounds. All have enjoyed the music (and the food that seems to be a part of any activity we hold). Many have found that they share other interests as well. Topics we've explored have run the gamut: making a gingerbread house, smart investing, fly fishing, American Girl crafts and cooking with edible flowers.

As a new library, we don't yet qualify for state aid. We're open for a few hours six days each week. We receive many book donations, including an increasing number of memorial and honor books. We have under 20,000 volumes in our collection, but we've budgeted to increase the number of new books each month. A donated computer and free Internet access provide additional service to the community, but we realize we're woefully behind in terms of technology. Considering everything we don't have, it's surprising that our biggest problem is a lack of space.

Fund raising is always a priority. We run small projects throughout the year, and we hold an annual auction which generates several thousand dollars each year. About half the money goes for operating expenses and new books. We're saving the balance, trying to establish the fund that can sustain the Weatherly Area Community Library.

Right now, the library depends on the dedication of a small group of volunteers. But we're confident that it will create its own new supporters. The same love of books, reading and libraries that pushed us into forming the library is a force that inspires people of all ages and backgrounds. Now that the library exists, it will be a magnet for others who feel the same way. We're looking forward to getting to know them, and seeing the library grow under their care.

Library Services in Montserrat: Helping People Realize Their Full Potential

Gracelyn Cassell

Gracelyn Cassell worked as the librarian in the public library of Montserrat from 1982 to 1987 and is now Librarian III in the acquisitions division of the main library of the University of the West Indies, Mona Campus, Kingston, Jamaica.

Undoubtedly, I have been a painful disappointment to my father who had dreams of a career for me in the medical field. He is still trying to understand why I lost interest in helping the wounded and decided instead on librarianship for a profession. But I still remember what led to my decision to become a librarian.

I was a 16-year-old student working on a research project. The librarian, who would later become my boss and friend, knew about the project. So when I fell sick and had to stay home in bed, she sent me some material and I was able to continue working from home. I had not asked for this service but she had decided that it was the thing to do. I was ecstatic. I was sold. I thought it would be wonderful to have a career which anticipated people's information needs and tried to respond to them. I wanted badly to be a librarian.

The time came to apply for a scholarship and I remember the government's personnel officer insisting that I forget librarianship because the scholarships on offer were for studies in the sciences. My response was thanks but no, it was librarianship for me or nothing. I have no idea what happened but one week after the term had started at the University of the West Indies, Mona Campus, Kingston, Jamaica, I was advised that I would get a scholarship and that I had to hurry off immediately for Jamaica.

I turned up at Mona and duly registered for the B.A. in Library Studies and so began a love affair with a Jamaica which stimulated ideas of what could be done through libraries to help people be all that they can be. I still have programmes from the many plays, music recitals, dance performances and exhibitions that I attended over the three-year period. And my every thought during that time was how much better life in Montserrat would be if only people had the kind of exposure I was getting.

I remember weeping bitterly at a friend's graveside shortly after I had graduated in 1982. During my time in Kingston, Clifford and I had spent many an evening outside my dormitory discussing what we would do on returning to Montserrat. But when he graduated from the School of Art in Kingston, the effort was simply too much for his system, which had struggled with the effects of rheumatic fever over the years, and he died.

I cried because we had dreams of cooperative efforts for improving the understanding and appreciation of all kinds of art in Montserrat. In my dreams of dynamic library services, I had envisioned him as the resource person for art workshops sponsored by the Montserrat Public Library. So, I was left to implement the plans without the practical and artistic strength my friend Clifford would have provided.

Back in Montserrat

Having discovered that a Peace Corps volunteer I met soon after returning home knew calligraphy, I coerced him into doing a library workshop. None of the supplies required for this were available on the island but a quick telephone call to his father in the United States had calligraphy pens and ink arriving by courier as a gift to the library. It was my first effort at organizing a skills workshop and my expectations were not high. It was a pleasant surprise therefore to see the interest and enthusiasm that the workshop generated. Those who came were serious about learning this new skill and we offered them their pens as gifts. This would be the first of many skills training workshops I would help implement.

At a meeting held in St. Kitts, I had the good fortune to meet two dynamic adult educators. When I returned to Montserrat, I started discussions to bring them to Montserrat to do a workshop with adult educators on the island. Through the government's development unit, I was able to secure funds from a donor agency. The two were able to serve as facilitators at a week-long workshop co-hosted by the public library and the University of the West Indies, School of Continuing Studies. Volunteers working in the prison, retired teachers helping high school dropouts and others teaching formal classes attended this workshop on the adult learner. We followed the participatory approach, which is the hallmark of educator Paulo Freire's work, and that participants were hearing about for the first time. They returned to their work with new fire.

Early on I also became involved in archival work. When I first joined the public library, Father Jay Dobbin was busy researching his book on the Jombie Dance. He needed to use the archival material previously housed in the basement of the governor's official residence. It so happened that the governor of the day had an interest in libraries and archives and he thought that the public library should supervise the use of this material. In the past, researchers had been allowed to use the collection without any supervision whatsoever. A listing done in 1965 showed that some of the material had since gone missing. The library's role was to organize the material to facilitate use. Of course we set about doing this as librarians rather than as archivists. So instead of organizing the collection into series of records, we listed each piece as an entity. There were over 2,500 pieces; files, bound volumes, some fragile, some fading but together they provided a picture of how government activities and decisions affected the life of the people of Montserrat.

I joined the team in sorting and listing these documents, some of them dating back to the 1800s. Initially, progress was slow because we were fascinated by what we were reading. We were seeing island history from a perspective totally different from what history texts of the day would ever throw light on. I saw workable projects which were submitted by farsighted people only to have them shelved because the colonial government did not consider the projects to be self-sustaining. There were stories of ordinary men and women whom we knew and who played significant roles in the development of the island; they were the island's unsung heroes. As a result of this exercise, I became interested in conducting oral history interviews. There were people in the community who were living examples of island stories. I had to make an effort to capture as many of these stories as I could before these people passed on.

Oral Histories and Puppetry

By 1984, I was well on my way with this project of collecting oral histories. I was going out in the evenings, tape recorder in hand, visiting anyone who was over 70 years of age. It was a fascinating time. The stories brought to life another time in Montserrat's history, its culture and folklore; injustices meted out because people lacked the wherewithal to fight for their rights; the struggles people endured to make a living in an unfavorable economic climate. Some of the stories were heartrending. But there is a resilience in the people of Montserrat, particularly the older folk, who seem able to deal with all that life throws their way without losing their ability to laugh at themselves.

Some of the folktales and folkways have been incorporated in a children's book, *And I Remember Many Things: Folklore of the Caribbean*, which was published in 1992. Using another transcript of an interview with a gentleman who has since died, I was able to coordinate what he said with what was written in the archival record. This is reported in an unpublished paper entitled ?A Turbulent Time: The Thomas Sugar Story."

One folktale, "Anancy and Brer Terecuma," was developed into a script for the library's first puppet show. A CUSO volunteer, Douglas, whose hobby was making puppets and marionettes and staging shows, was co-opted, this time to train library staff. It was part of our preparation for one of our Children's Library Annual Summer Programmes (CLASP), which the library had been hosting since 1988.

We started out learning how to make hand puppets. Then, Douglas wanted a story we could use for the puppet show and I went back to my tapes and transcripts and chose an Anancy folktale. We worked on the script and the music to go with it and Douglas built the stage. Many of the children and adults in the audience were seeing their first puppet show when they attended the closing exercises for that year's summer program.

Then we went on to marionettes. It was the Christmas of 1989. Not much was planned for the Christmas festivities because people were still recovering from the devastation of Hurricane Hugo. A Montserratian, Henry Greenaway, who had been living in the United States, returned with a lot of energy and wanted to do a benefit concert. We agreed that it was an opportunity for the Alliouagana Library Friends to raise funds for future summer programmes. (Alliouagana, or land of the prickly bush, was the name the Amerindians had given to Montserrat.) It would be a variety concert with children performing. The show brought the house down and alas the stage as well. As the performing marionettes returned to take their final bow, the stage originally built for the puppet show, and which had been made taller for the marionette show, tumbled down with this last act leaving Douglas and me feeling exposed as we were perched on the table.

Archives Training

The early foraging into the cellar of archives was also responsible for my interest in archives and their value in understanding history. In 1986, a Commonwealth scholarship allowed me to go to the University College of London's School of Library, Archive and Information Studies. The College of London offered a master's program in overseas archives studies. While I was away in London, the Permanent Secretary for Development decided that the slightly larger room housing the Documentation Centre would better serve as an office for one of his economists. He would have all of his staff near him. Prisoners were duly called out, as was and still is the custom, to deal with emptying the room, but no one informed the library staff.

So, I returned in 1987 to find that the Documentation Centre, which had been my responsibility, was now a mass of garbage bags and boxes of books on the floor of a much smaller room next door to the men's toilet. The room was on the ground floor. Two years later this became a blessing in disguise.

Uncomplainingly, I spent those first weeks after my return from the United Kingdom reorganizing. I reduced the 100-plus pages of my M.A. thesis, "Records Management Programme for the Government of Montserrat: An Implementation Plan," into an eight-page proposal to the government with the hope that an archival programme with the required legal support would be implemented. Unfortunately, that proposal would be pulled out with each successive government and without anything happening to further archival development in Montserrat. Nor would there be any official recognition of two subsequent proposals for digitizing the extremely fragile material in the small archival collection held by the library. I keep being reminded of somebody's cynical comment that it is only with independence that governments show any interest in the development of their archives.

While I reviewed the correspondence files in the library office, to find out what had been going on during my year's absence, I discovered a letter which had been sent by a professor then at Harvard University. His research led him to request access to the Deed Books of Montserrat. Despite the fact that the letter was almost a year old, I decided to respond to it. Out of that developed a project, funded by Harvard University, that made use of experts from the Antigua Archives who were microfilming several Deed Books in the courthouse. These are the only copies of Montserrat archival material on microfilm that the library has to date.

The Montserrat Public Library

I continued coordinating Montserrat's involvement in a number of regional information systems. People were doing interesting projects with alternative energy sources and they were linked with the Caribbean Energy Information System based in Jamaica. Others had products they wanted to develop and package and they would be directed to CARIRI, the Caribbean Industrial Research Institute in Trinidad. When we had requests for information we were unable to supply, we made telephone calls or sent faxes to CARISPLAN, the Caribbean Information System for Social and Economic Planning in Trinidad, or to OECS INFONET, the Organization of Eastern Caribbean

States Information Network. Material would arrive by courier or by the kind hand of someone traveling to Montserrat.

There was no denying that the Montserrat Public Library had changed. With not much more space than that available in 1951, when free library services replaced the subscription service offered since 1890, people who once did not dare enter the library would meet me on the street and discuss their projects and I would try to link them with a relevant source of information. I often reminded the skeptics that the small collection in the library had little to do with our potential to get them the information they required. We had links with regional and international organizations which had bigger collections. These were the networks I would use to get material quickly in response to information requests. I got great satisfaction from seeing the users happy with timely service. In a newspaper article once, the editor included the library as one of the places where staff were helpful, efficient and customer oriented. I don't know how much that had to do with him occasionally calling me out of bed to get information from the library for his weekly paper!

Hurricanes and Volcanoes

After September 17, 1989, Montserrat was a changed place. On the 18th when the rains abated after Hurricane Hugo had devastated the island, I ventured out to see what had happened to family friends and workplace. All communication lines were down. The trek into Plymouth necessitated climbing over tree trunks, utility poles, pieces of roofs, broken furniture and other debris. The library was one of the first stops. And, yes, the door which I had specifically but unsuccessfully asked the Public Works Department to secure had been blown away. The library was swamped with four inches of water. A cursory glance was enough for me to decide that the damaged material could be salvaged with quick action. The roof over the Documentation Centre was damaged but the ground floor collection was protected from water damage and exposure to the over 200 mile-per-hour winds.

The death toll, fortunately, was low, but the devastation was widespread. I knew that people would be trying to pull the remnants of their lives together. Since my basement flat had sustained little damage, it was up to me to start the restoration work at the library until the other members of staff could join me. During those first days, the only thing that could be done was to try to clear the floor of the water that had seeped in. The hurricane had left lots of rain in its wake and each morning before I could start working on the damaged material, I would sweep out gallons of water coming in from a gaping hole in the roof of the adjoining government headquarters. Pleas to the Public Works Department to put a cover over this hole fell on ears deaf to library needs. All energies were spent helping homeowners secure what was left of their houses.

Some days later, staff started trickling into work. The sun appeared to grateful cheers and we put reading tables outside and spread out the books to dry. Lysol, an insecticidal and anti-mold spray, and rolls of white paper towels were our only tools to prevent mold growth and pages sticking together. The library's greatest book losses were not caused by damage to the building itself but to the homes of the users who were unable to secure their library books. However, once people saw us at work out in the open, they started bringing in damp books, some worth saving, others too far gone.

Each year we planned CLASP, the Children's Library Annual Summer Programme, with its overall theme of "Our Country, Our People, Our Future." Its objectives were to heighten awareness in youngsters to environmental and cultural concerns as well as to encourage reading. We lamented not having our own space for the program. Each year, it was a veritable feat of moving materials, furniture and equipment to a church hall in the first year and various other schools afterwards. We had to rearrange the programme schedule and plans to deal with shortcomings in the buildings we used. We learned the prudence of trying electrical outlets before assuming that there was electricity in a room.

In spite of the many difficulties, we did manage over an eight-year period to host seven summer programmes. The very first one was our smallest and the sub-theme was "Our Island." The Caribbean Conservation Association in Barbados, using material we had pulled together, sponsored and produced "Our Land and People," the first of several videos which resulted from these programmes. The following year we looked at "Our Forests" only to see them denuded by the fury of Hurricane Hugo. In 1990, we turned to "Our Water Resources" and another video was produced in conjunction with staff from the Montserrat Water Authority and the Agricultural Department. In subsequent years we had programmes on saving the beaches, the Amerindian Heritage, the impact of garbage on Montserrat and the importance of recycling.

It was in 1995 that we were able to pull out the 1993 theme which had been shelved because our energies were concentrated on moving the library from the soon to be demolished government headquarters to the second floor of a commercial building. Our planning for the programme with the sub-theme "Our African Heritage" was going well until we were within a fortnight of the day. The long dormant Soufriere Hills volcano roared to life and caused an exodus of people including many of our resource persons. We were tempted to shelve the programme once again but the government thought we would be providing an opportunity for the remaining youngsters to forget the crisis which was affecting everyone's life. We spent many a time gazing at the mountain, hoping against hope, that we would not be forced to deal with evacuating children to the north of Plymouth. Fortunately, we were spared having to put evacuation drills into practice and we breathed a sigh of relief when the programme came to an end with the closing performance of drumming demonstrations, modeling of tie-dye wraps made by the children, and storytelling.

It was to be the last summer program of its kind, ending an era of community involvement for activities ranging from the writing of theme songs, the production of videos to the presentation of lectures, all with generous sponsorship from the private sector. Field trips took the children around the island to parts now covered by hundreds of tons of volcanic material. The bus drivers on these field trips claimed that the information, which was an important part of these trips, was also useful for them in their interaction with tourists.

Not long after, the island was on red alert. On August 21, Plymouth and other areas had to be evacuated. It would be the first of three evacuations, the last of which crushed our dreams of occupying a new library. (This attractive building lies under several feet of ash in Plymouth.) Nobody in our parent ministry, the Ministry of Education, Health and Community Services, was able to tell us where the library was to move to. We begged the Minister of Education to secure the old stone building which housed Salem Community Library run by volunteers as a relocation point for the public library. We lost out to the prison ministry, which moved the prisoners among the love stories and other works of fiction on the shelves.

We knew that we did not want to leave irreplaceable material to be burned in an eruption. At that point we were worried that the entire island might be consumed, but the meteorologists kept assuring us that the north was relatively safe. We sat down and went through the names of people who lived in the north and who had basement storage space. The first person we called agreed to house, for a short period and at no cost, the more than 15 boxes of material that we had prepared. It was only a matter of organizing transportation and help for lifting. With a pass from the authorities to go back into the unsafe zone, we made our way into Plymouth with many a glance up to the mountains to see what was happening.

My small patio became the gathering area for library staff still trying to resettle in the northern safe zone. We drove around trying to find anyplace that would provide space for our material but everything was already reserved. Then I realized that my neighbor's unfinished house with its roof and windows could serve as a storage for the materials. We could then work on offering some form of mobile service to users.

But before this could be arranged, we were visited by hurricanes Luis and Marilyn on September 4 and 15, respectively. With shelters bursting at the seams, scientists gave the government the all-clear for all evacuated areas except

Long Ground in close proximity to the volcanic activity. People eagerly returned to their homes and we were happy to have a library from which to operate. There was some water damage to the building but our precautionary measures protected the material. We left our valuable archival and local history material in storage because we were told that the volcanic crisis, though subdued, was certainly not at an end.

We were able to rent the unfinished house, and the government installed water and electricity, and this has been the relocated library since the final evacuation in April 1996. The limited space necessitated leaving behind two thirds of the collection. From time to time we made daring runs back into Plymouth to get material required by users. An old and leaking school bus was temporarily used for taking materials to shelters and for collecting material from users. It was not a happy solution. Use statistics took a nose dive, partly a result of the thousands who left the island.

At the end of 1996, the government provided the library with a multimedia system and Internet access. Information technology took on added importance for a number of reasons. Reference works on CD-ROM compensated for the multi-volume works left behind. We considered that staff constraints would also affect library services and we negotiated for a cataloging package which would eliminate the need for most original cataloging. Information from the Internet on mobile services helped us prepare a project proposal to acquire a bookmobile.

Although I have been made redundant (those on leave without pay were asked to return by August 1997 or be made redundant), I still maintain my contacts with the staff of the Montserrat Public Library. I remember when I graduated being asked by a Jamaican library whether I thought it was the right thing for me to go back to that small library on that tiny island. For a while that question haunted me. But now that I'm working in an academic library which is a lot bigger than the Montserrat Public Library, I know I made the right choice then. I had the opportunity to work with colleagues who helped me to grow and who knew what it was to work as a team. In a smaller system, one has more control over end products. In the bigger system, there is specialization.

The wide network of professional colleagues and supportive friends that I have developed over the years has resulted mainly from the numerous workshops and conferences I was privileged to attend as Montserrat's representative. I'm now one of 22 librarians. Opportunities to do what I did in the past will be limited but there are also opportunities to be involved in new activities. Now, as a little fish in a bigger pond, I continue to strengthen my supportive network through electronic mail. I have had guidance, gift donations and encouragement in my work from the user groups on the Internet that I joined. This is an exciting and challenging period of witnessing the implementation of automation processes, of learning new procedures and contributing to improvements in procedure.

I do not know if I was born to be a librarian but it certainly has been a rewarding career choice, and I think that one day my father will appreciate the joy and satisfaction I get from my work.

The Resource Centre Experience in South Africa: An Important Contribution to Librarianship

Faye Reagon

Faye Reagon is finishing her master's degree in Library and Information Studies at the University of Cape Town (UCT, South Africa), and will continue her studies on the doctoral level. She plans to do her doctorate thesis on the changing role of community libraries in the context of the information society in developing countries.

Introduction

The situation regarding libraries in South Africa has always been a complex one. While they compare favorably with those in many advanced Western countries, South African libraries have always been steeped in the apartheid tradition of segregation and inequity. There is clear evidence indicating that information provision in South Africa was historically organized purely on racial lines, where a white[1] minority had access to the wealth of information resources such as books, buildings and technology (Kalley, 1995: 199; Karlsson; 1992: 7; Karelse, 1991: 4; NEPI; 1992: 30). These conditions were always challenged from within the anti-apartheid movement, and in the early 1980s many community organizations responded by developing "Resource Centres" as alternative structures to the formal library system. These Resource Centres operated in different ways and had very different agendas from mainstream libraries.

This essay, based on a broader study on information provision to developing communities in South Africa, intends to revisit the concept of Resource

Centres as an alternative library model and to investigate whether it has indeed been able to impact on library and information services (LIS)[2] in the post-apartheid South Africa. Though the methodology for this study includes the use of the literature as well as discussions with individuals, it is important to note that the author draws from firsthand experience as a political activist and a Resource Centre activist during the 1980s and early 1990s.

The concept of Resource Centres is not a new phenomenon in librarianship. Indeed, much has been written about this in the international literature. We have witnessed activity in this area for nearly four decades and it was as long ago as 1968 when library practitioners in parts of Africa lobbied for low-cost, widespread library services for accessibility to local village communities and worked closely with those engaged in adult education and literacy (Rosenberg, 1993:29).

In the South African context, however, Resource Centres took on a new meaning due to their location within the struggle against apartheid. Because of their origin, Resource Centres acquired an autonomous character with a very distinctive discourse and use of terminology. Examples of this is the use of "Resource Centre movement" as opposed to "library and information service" and "Resource Centre activist" as opposed to "librarian" or "information worker."

Describing a typical Resource Centre, one Resource Centre activist fondly remembers "a single room, or a set of rooms usually doubling up as a meeting room, containing periodicals, newspapers, Roneo Machines, silk-screening facilities, a television and video machine and some shelves with a variety of books. The walls were bright with posters of an anti-apartheid nature…. What struck one was its vibrancy…. It was a hive of activity from early in the morning to late at night" (Daniels, 1994: 34). Karlsson and Booi (1993: 2) provide a more formal definition of a Resource Centre:

> A space or building in which human and other resources in a variety of media (e.g., books, journals, newspapers, film, slides, video and audio cassettes, three dimensional objects, etc.) and equipment (e.g., recorders, cameras, computers, photocopiers, printers, fax machines, etc.) are arranged or made accessible in an appropriate manner for the purpose of empowering people through information dissemination, production, skills and resource sharing.

Resource Centres are not homogeneous and can be distinguished according to the function they perform. Karelse (1991: 3) identifies three types: 1. Community Resource Centres, i.e., those which are geographically based in residential areas and which provide information to the community at large; 2. Aligned Resource Centres, which are in-house and perform a support role to a broader organization; and 3. Autonomous Resource Centres, which play a similar role to aligned resource centres but function independently. The latter two have a targeted audience and have some degree of specialization.

Historical Development

The struggle for democracy in South Africa reached a turning point towards the end of the 1970s. It was characterized by the emergence of the mass organizations (later to be called the Mass Democratic Movement [MDM]), an alliance of trade unions and community-based organizations such as youth and student organizations, civic associations and women's groups. These groups transformed the nature of politics in the country. It was during this period that new types of non-governmental organizations (NGO) emerged. Commonly known as service organizations, these institutions arose as part of a strategy to advance and strengthen organizations within the MDM by providing them with services and resources. Repressive conditions such as censorship and the prohibition of a number of organizations within the MDM led to an increased reliance on service organizations. The inadequate provision of library and information facilities and the lack of relevant information were fast becoming burning issues and service organizations responded by developing Resource Centres. These organizations were never short of funding with money pouring in from all corners of the world—from international donor organizations and churches—who were all willing to help the disenfranchised in South Africa.

The Nature of Resource Centres

Although a typology of Resource Centres was introduced earlier in the chapter, the following features indicate their distinctive nature:

- They aligned themselves with organizations that aimed to overthrow the apartheid regime.
- They shared a common goal to build and strengthen mass based organizations that operated within disadvantaged communities.
- They shared a common culture of democracy and the promotion of democratic practice through their work.
- They saw themselves as being accountable to the broader community they served.
- They saw themselves as playing an educational role and as facilitators within the non-formal education framework.
- They were non-governmental organizations and as such were not part of the established library and information services infrastructure.
- They were not funded by the state but rather by donor organizations and church groups.

- They were critical of the existing library and information system and supported its transformation.

METHODOLOGY EMPLOYED

The strength of Resource Centres lay in their progressive methodologies. They were characterized by: a) their vision to empower disadvantaged communities; b) their close relationship with the users they served; and c) their approach to information work, which differed distinctly from that of traditional libraries. Resource Centres moved beyond mere information provision and actively sought to empower users by acting as facilitators and catalysts. This role reflected their educational nature—emphasizing the intimacy between libraries and education. They supported the notion of "Peoples' Education" and adopted the methodologies of many leading educationalists such as Freire and La Belle.

RESOURCES

An extensive list of media forms were kept including books, manuals, periodicals, pamphlets, conference papers and reports, reference works, posters, maps and charts, toys, videos, films, slides, slide-tape programmes, photographs, multi-media resource packages, banners, T-shirts, stickers, badges and electronic databases (Karlsson and Booi, 1993: 27). Their book collection consisted of works that were not readily available on the shelves in the formal public library system, the Centres' focus being mainly left-wing works relating to the socio-economic and political situation and the struggle in South Africa. The book collections of the aligned and independent Resource Centres reflected the primary function of the parent organization.

Equipment was offered as a resource in many Resource Centres. Karlsson and Booi (1993: 28) mentions the commonly-used equipment such as televisions, videocassette recorders, photocopiers, computers and printers, overhead projectors, tape recorders, typewriters and fax machines. Some Resource Centres even kept document binders, guillotines, button-making machines, public address systems, megaphones, sewing machines, bicycles, carpentry tools, etc. But resources were not only limited to documents and equipment. Resource Centre staff with their talents as publishers, authors, teachers and trainers proved to be a valuable resource.

GOVERNANCE AND FUNDING

Issues such as democracy, accountability and transparency were taken seriously in the management and functioning of the organization. They were not state-subsidized and relied on funding from donor organizations at home and abroad. Regular, painstaking attempts were made to raise funds themselves through cake sales, curry and rice evenings, and raffles.

INFRASTRUCTURE

As Resource Centres mushroomed in different parts of the country, they began organizing themselves into structures to encourage debate and discussion around common issues. Regional forums like the following were formed: The Inter Resource Forum (Western Cape), The Natal Resource Centre Forum, The Transvaal Resource Centre Network, The Transkei Fieldworkers Network and the Border Services Resource Centre Forum.

STAFFING

Few Resource Centres employed qualified staff and this created the need for systematic training. Training courses were developed by service organizations such as The Community Resource Centre Training Project (CRCTP), SACHED Trust and ERIP amongst many others. Academics from library schools at universities were engaged. Special focus was given to the basic skills needed to manage a library. Examples of these are cataloguing and classification, repackaging of information, financial management, basic computer skills, report writing, and so forth.

The Significance of Resource Centres

While Resource Centres emerged in a specific historical context, one cannot dispute that they have contributed significantly to the formal library and information system. As a phenomenon, the movement attracted the attention of many practitioners and academics within the library discipline and the Resource Centre was often cited as a model for public libraries in the new South Africa. It is not possible, however, to measure the achievements of the Resource Centre movement by indicators and standards normally used within traditional library services as their objectives, methodologies and philosophies differ considerably.

Because of their special nature, Resource Centres demonstrate a new approach to information provision. They encapsulate the essence of proactivity and vigour, introducing a new dimension to the library scene. Their close relationship with the communities they serve and their democratic nature serve as crucial pointers to those concerned with community librarianship in South

Africa about the need for public libraries to be imbedded within the experiences of communities. This new ethos affirms the importance of being more attuned to grassroots needs and emphasizes the importance of participation and accountability.

But, the richness of the achievements of Resource Centres is not only restricted to the methodologies used in information provision. They were also a significant force in raising issues that exceeded the boundaries of academic discourse, especially concerning the role of the public library system that placed librarianship in a socio-political context. They introduced concepts and terms which were new to traditional librarianship—concepts such as development, reconstruction, transformation, accountability, transparency, democracy and so forth.

Key contributors to this discourse were progressives[3] within the formal library sector who not only supported the well being of Resource Centres but challenged the existing orthodoxy. They challenged traditionalists within the LIS sector to be more analytical and more critical of the situation they found themselves in. They criticized the failure of the formal library sector to challenge the state on its apartheid policies and they pointed to the neglect of issues pertaining to black library workers.

Resource Centres in a Crisis

The problem of sustainability is not new to libraries, especially those in Africa. By the start of the 1990s many Resource Centres started folding and their numbers decreased rapidly. In 1992 the *Resource Centre Directory* (1992: 3) recorded the existence of 120 Resource Centres. By 1998, the *Prodder Directory* recorded only 20 (HSRC, 1999). This crisis, shared by many NGOs in South Africa, was exacerbated by the decline of funding from external agencies. Viennings (1993: 513), suggests that this decline may be related to new funding criteria that no longer attached importance to anti-apartheid activity. South Africa was now competing with NGOs in Eastern Europe making it more difficult to secure funds.

But the crisis in which Resource Centres found themselves did not stem only from the lack of funds. A large part could be attributed to the absence of a clear and decisive leadership—one that was committed, consistent and equal to their task. In most instances, the Centres were staffed by unqualified political activists who worked on a voluntary basis and could not focus specifically on the tasks at hand. Resource Centres were weakened even further by the continuous flow of staff in and out of the organization.

But according to Daniels (1994: 35) the overarching reason for this crisis was the transformation process the country was involved in at the time.

This process, characterized by a period of negotiation and compromise and coupled with the willingness to merge different cultures, histories and understandings, impacted much on the structures concerned with libraries. Many formal public library services recognized the need for change and were already becoming proactive in this regard. Since they had in place a well-established infrastructure and the needed resources to take forward a new public library system, they were drawn more and more into the plans of the politicians. Resource Centres on the other hand did not feature much in this new scenario and to a large extent became marginalized, like many progressives within the LI sector. This assertion is supported by Maria Farelo, the national coordinator of the Library and Information Workers Organization (LIWO), who comments:

> The government, instead of looking to democratic structures to spearhead changes in LIS structures today, has asked individuals, very often who have no background or credibility in the progressive LIS world, to head LIS committees [LIWO Conference, 1995: 1].

The comments made by Rosenberg perhaps best explain the future of Resource Centres. Predicting their life cycle to be about two years she justifies this by saying that "their birth is followed by rapid growth and a good deal of local publicity and attention. This is followed by a period of slow decline, accompanied by theft, the departure of the initiators, loss of interest amongst staff and users—the library still exists but signs of life are barely discernible" (Rosenberg, 1993: 34).

While this very contentious view may be criticized, it provides us with an honest comment and perhaps very aptly reflects the realities.

The Post-Apartheid Era

South Africa has recently enjoyed its second democratic election. While many milestones have been reached in other sectors of society, anecdotal evidence suggests that in many aspects the library information sector remains untransformed. The Resource Centre movement of the eighties has crumbled, and the formal public library sector has, instead, claimed its space as the mainstream in community librarianship. But the situation has not changed much. Libraries are placed low on the priority list of cash-strapped local authorities, leaving little room for innovation and change. They also continue to be managed by the old guard who lack a clear vision and the confidence to guide the sector through the transitional period. The values and insights gained through the Resource Centre experience have not been transmitted to present day public library practice. Nor has their vision of an appropriate service become the dominant paradigm.

It is clear that public libraries will have the capacity to play a positive role only when they have transformed themselves into relevant structures. Their relevancy will be determined by the type of vision they project—a vision which ensures the creation of an equitable information order; promotes life-long learning; appreciates the notion of community ownership and accountability; supports the development of an Information Community[4] in South Africa; and takes into account the lessons learned through the Resource Centre experience.

These conditions are absolutely vital to the achievement of a new public library system. Such a system is in keeping with library models currently being implemented in other parts of the world, particularly in Malaysia, Singapore and the United Kingdom. A new paradigm has emerged in librarianship globally which shifts away from the traditional library model to one that emphasizes the usefulness of libraries and enhances accessibility.

Multi-Purpose Community Centres (MPCCs)

The few Resource Centres that have survived no longer focus on their initial objectives. They have changed their role to adapt to the new conditions prevailing in the post-apartheid South Africa. They have shifted from "protest politics" to reconstruction and development issues. A recent unpublished survey conducted by the author found many Centres have become "next generation" Resource Centres, or rather, Multi-Purpose Community Centres (MPCCs)[5] (Reagon, 1999: 33).

Described as "a structure which enables communities to manage their own development, by providing access to appropriate information, facilities, resources, training and services," MPCCs continue to address the information needs of communities. Only now there is more emphasis on new information and communication technologies (ICTs) and issues associated with the emerging information society (National Information and Technology Forum, 1998: 7). Their interest in information provision is noted in a survey conducted by the National Information and Technology Forum (NITF) where it emerged that 45 percent of the targeted MPCCs included a library/resource centre as part of their services (Nassimbeni, 1999:159).

But it is questionable whether we can depend on MPCCs as a solution. As yet they are not self-sustaining units and like Resource Centres earlier on, they rely much on the tender mercies of donor organizations who tend only to support the "flavor of the month" issues. They will share the same fate as Resource Centres unless they are incorporated into the mainstream as information providers and, like other government structures, are a priority in government expenditure. The government, however, has underscored the designing of appropriate structures to serve the diverse needs of communities and at a recent conference has identified MPCCs as a delivery agent.[6]

The message received from this is that the government has dismissed public libraries as an important player and has instead looked to others to play this role. It would make far more sense for the government to support the transformation of public libraries in South Africa into structures that will benefit all as opposed to spending time, money and energy on the development of parallel structures.

I support the notion that public libraries should be developed into the meaningful and relevant structures once envisaged of the MPCC. As information providers, they clearly occupy a niche within the information environment. This can be justified with the following: a) the public library performs an enabling role particularly because it is one of the agents that supports life-long learning and empowerment; b) public libraries have traditionally been charged with the role of information provider to communities and have accumulated a wealth of knowledge and expertise in this area; c) they have in place the needed infrastructure and resources to carry out the tasks required; and d) they have, in their employ a host of qualified and trained personnel who are able to carry out the skilled tasks normally associated with information provision.

The development of public policy in South Africa is not clear cut and it is up to library and information workers to play a proactive role in guiding politicians in making correct decisions. They should seize the opportunity presented by the MPCCs and, with other stakeholders, must carve out a new public library system—one that is relevant and that is owned by the community.

Endnotes

1. The terms "white," "colored," "African" and "Indian" refer to statutory race classifications in South Africa prior to April 1994. The latter three refer to the disenfranchised sections that throughout this chapter will be referred to as "black."

2. Library and information services (LIS) refers to the broad range of library services in South Africa including the national library, community libraries, government libraries, university and college libraries and special libraries.

3. This term in used extensively in the South African anti-apartheid literature. It is a term which refers to those who form part of the left of the political spectrum.

4. The Information Community incorporates a vision "that seeks to shift the emphasis of the advantages offered by the information revolution towards a fuller balance between individuals and social groups, communities and society" (Benjamin, 1998: 6).

5. An MPCC is a type of Telecentre. A Telecentre is defined as "a location which

facilitates and encourages the provision of a wide variety of public and private information-based goods and services, and which supports local economic and social development. Such services include basic communication such as voice, fax, email, Internet access, etc; public and quasi-public services such as telemedicine, distance education, municipal government services, training, access to information on markets, crops and weather conditions and much more" (Acacia, 1999: 1). The use of Telecentres as a tool is supported by G7 countries and UNESCO.

6. The conference, held in 1996, was called the Information Society and Development Conference (ISAD), and it was here that the government put together their framework for the development of an information society in South Africa.

Works Cited

Acacia Telecentre Page. (http://www.idrc.ca/acacia/telecentre.html.)

Benjamin, P. "Multi-Purpose Community Centres in South Africa." *Meta-Info Bulletin 8* (1998). (http://www.librarynet.co.za/Meta-Info_bulletin8.htm.)

Daniels, G. "Resource Centres: A Challenge for Us All." *Cape Librarian* (January 1994): 34–35.

HSRC. *Prodder Directory* (1999). (http://www.amandla.org/za/host/advres.html.)

Kalley, J. "Community libraries in a South African Township: The Alexandra Experience." *South African Journal of Library and Information Science* 63.4 (1995): 199–205.

Karelse, C. M. "The Role of Resource Centres in Building a Democratic Non-Racial and United South Africa." *Innovation* 3 (1991): 3–8.

Karlsson, J. "Resource Centres: Branding Tongs or Tapas?" Unpublished paper presented at the SAILIS Annual Conference, Vereeniging, 1992.

_____, and N. Booi. "Resource Centres in South Africa." *Innovation* 5 (1993): 27–29.

Lor, P. "Memorandum on the State of Libraries in South Africa." *The LIASA Letter* 2.1 (1998): 7–12.

Media Resource Centre. Directory of South African Resource Centres. Durban: 1992.

Nassimbeni, M. "The Information Society in South Africa: From Global Origins to Local Vision." *South African Journal of Library and Information Science* 66.4 (1999): 154–160.

National Information and Technology Forum. *Multi-Purpose Community Centre: Research Report* (1998). (http://wn.apc.org/nitf/mpcc.)

NEPI. *Library and Information Services: Report of the NEPI Library and Information Services Research Group.* Cape Town: Oxford UP, 1992.

Reagon, F. *Improving Public Library Services: Using Multi-Purpose Community Centres (MPCCs).* Unpublished Masters Dissertation, 1999.

Rosenberg, D. "Rural Community Resource Centres: A Sustainable Option for Africa." *Information Development* 9.1/2 (1993): 29–35.

Viennings, T. "The Relationship Between Resource Centres and Non-Formal Education." *Proceedings of the Africa Nova Conference.* Vol. 2, 3–7 (May 1994): 512–517.

Of Libraries

Carey Harrison

Carey Harrison is currently Bernard H. Stern Professor of Humor at Brooklyn College of the City University of New York. He is the author of numerous scripts for stage, screen, radio and television.

Libraries!—I was barely conscious of libraries until I was a college student in Britain and made my way to that fearsome, ugly building, the Cambridge University Library. Until then the public libraries so many teenagers fondly remember, places where early dreams were fed and exotic quests initiated, Ali Baba public libraries spilling jewels of knowledge ... these formed no part of my life. I was raised here in New York City, educated at Manhattan's Lycée Français (struggling with French books in our Germantown apartment) and then was sent to boarding school in Britain where the only books we knew were school books or books sent from home and the local public libraries were taboo, "out of bounds" like the towns and villages that held them.

Hence my terror when I bicycled up to the dreaded, dungeon-like U.L. at Cambridge, the echoing University Library. Somehow I had to find, on the shelves marked Practical Sciences (oh for the impractical ones!), the dusty tomes of 19th century excavation reports that first year archaeology students like myself were made to read, in an attempt to weed out the romantics among us and leave only those who understood that archaeology was hard, practical and unromantic. This project was a success in my case. So many books, so smelly, ancient, and hard to find when it was only one of them you wanted! Within a year my lifelong dreams of a career in archaeology lay ruined and buried as deep as any 19th century soil report. Libraries be praised! I changed to English, never looked back, and now, after 35 happy years as an author of fiction and with almost 200 plays and novels to my name I know how much

I owe to the dusty, dreary, grimly echoing awfulness of that university library! It put me off scholarship for a while.

My next acquaintance with a library was with London's dearest and most convivial library, the London Library, haunt of authors, readers, journalists and scholars alike. Its curious warren-like stacks with their vertiginous see-through walkways suspended on the iron fretwork of the floors—so that you see feet passing above you, clanging, and you appear to be treading on the heads of people below—have the unearthly afterlife feel of a Piranesi drawing stocked with books, or a circle of hell devoted to bibliomanes. But the sofa-strewn London Library reading room is as cozy as the most friendly ducal drawing-room of imagination—the perfect library setting. Having become an author, I now found I had to do just as much research as if I'd turned into the very thing I'd dreaded, a scholar dependent on research, and thus on dungeon-libraries. Happily the practice of fiction required research more various and a great deal less thorough than a scholar's.

But libraries it had to be. Eventually I wound up, as until recently all British writers did, at that fountainhead of library splendor, the British Museum. No one could surely have worked there, under the great umbrella of its ceiling (I like to think of Richard Rogers's Millennium Dome at Greenwich as a kind of memory trace or tribute to the old B.M. reading room), without in imagination glimpsing Karl Marx and a galaxy of his predecessors, the countless authors and savants who spent a great portion of their lives in that incomparably lovely room. Frequenting it cured me of my fear of libraries in a hurry. Not only scholars but notable contemporary novelists like Peter Ackroyd and Jonathan Coe, I found, used this majestic place as their daily "office."

Until, as I say, a few years ago. Now that the British Library is elsewhere, in the Euston Road, in that churlish piece of redbrick architecture of which Prince Charles rightly remarked that it looked a school for spies, where is there for a Briton—or any book-lover—to go for bibliophiliac inspiration? Where to feel the presence not only of books by the ton but ghostly booklovers by the century?

Trinity College, Dublin, has the most enchanting of all the world's libraries (visit the Book of Kells and you'll have the double-barreled bliss of an exit through the College Library), with its ancient busts interspersing the tall oaken stacks. But, truth to tell, the mantle of greatness falls on the New York Public Library, whose tradition is scarcely less glorious than that of the British Museum, in terms of its contribution to art and knowledge, and which sports a reading room which may not match the B.M.'s (what ever could?) but stands, refurbished, as a truly noble and gorgeous substitute.

I used to hate soup; soup and libraries, above all things. Now I must have grown up: I love them both, and have joined true book-lovers everywhere in cherishing those libraries that survive and in mourning above all other vanished buildings and all other vanished wonders of the world, the library at Alexandria. Even to dream, to speculate for a moment what books lost to us—what great authors entirely unknown to us!—it may have contained, is to enter a seductive parallel universe, and find oneself wandering the maze-like pages of a Jorge Luis Borges story.

And the library of the future? Pray God it might retain something of the tweedy, casual, sofa-strewn quality of the London Library, prizing an encouraging atmosphere in which to lose oneself in a book over the relentless efficiency of a literary fast-food delivery service. Beware the computer-driven world: in whose prophetic short story was it that a book-lover of the future went to his local, computer-run library and ordered *Kidnapped* by Robert Louis Stevenson, only to find himself arrested by the computer-fed police the following day, on suspicion of having kidnapped a person by the name of R.L. Stevenson?

I forget the author of this minatory, monitory tale, and there's a lesson even in that. It's the story, not the author, that survives, and so it should be. If all the covers and the spines and dust-jackets of the world were lost, what would it matter, so long as we had a library to hold the pages those lost covers once contained? This would be a literary world difficult to catalogue, it's true. But the stories would still be there, waiting for us, in the great maze, the great jungle, the great game that a library—see how far I've come?!—should be. Would Ali Baba's cave be a more potent dream if we imagined the riches it contained to have been filed by size and color? Hardly. Jewels spilling out of boxes, in every direction: isn't that still our over-riding image of riches, of surfeit, of excess? Of libraries, then: let them be surprising.

And let readers be, as I am now, patient. Let them grow up.

Libraries: The More They Change…

Michael Kahan

Michael Kahan teaches in the political science department at Brooklyn College of the City University of New York and has been a student and a university faculty member in the United States, England, Israel, and Australia.

The Francis Parkman Branch on Oakman Boulevard in Detroit is still a quiet haven of memory. My first live visit was sometime in the late 1940s, when I had enough confidence to pedal my bike across a busy avenue, and was brave enough to go alone into a new place, where I probably knew no one. It was a round-fronted, reddish-brick building with leaded Tudor windows and laced with climbing ivy. The inside was welcoming, in an official way. Bright sunshine spilled through the windows and gave a shimmer to the dust motes. Newspapers in racks lined one side of the front room, and a large reading table with high-backed wooden chairs around it took up most of the rest of the space. A librarian smiled at me from behind the front counter, which was piled high with books, some on display, others on their sides waiting to be re-shelved. I stopped in my tracks at the silence. I think I stayed only a short time that first visit.

Many years later, the summer after I graduated from high school and we were packing to move out of the house where I grew up, I found a dusty book in the basement, taken out many years before from the Francis Parkman Branch. My book? My brother's? I had no idea. I thought of the empty space on the library shelf where the book belonged, and of course I was nervous that this long-lost book might be traced to me. So, I made one last trip to that library, this time by car and at night when it would be closed. I slipped the book into the return slot next to the front door and heard it plop onto the bottom of the bin. I walked away, partly guilty and partly sad, but forever parted from the Francis Parkman Branch.

It wasn't that I had been totally faithful to this branch. There had been other libraries here and there. But the Francis Parkman was my first, certainly the first I had encountered on my own, and it had been my steady for quite a while. There had been, for example, the downtown branch, behind the J. L. Hudson department store, where my mother would sometimes stash me while she went shopping. There I met the only stern librarian of my youth: she told me in clear terms which parts of the library were not available to young people—unlike the Parkman Branch or the school library, which were unrestricted.

By the time I graduated from high school, my relationship with the Francis Parkman Branch had gone through many phases, and in the end we had settled on being good friends. At one stage, probably around the seventh grade, it had become my crowd's social club. Before we were allowed to "go out"—before we could drive cars on dates and park on dark streets afterward—we would arrange to meet at the library's large study tables, rendezvous in the stacks, and conspire in the bathrooms. We even did some homework there on occasion. In those days before the electronic revolution, it was our Web. We chatted, gossiped, and scoured the stacks for the unusual, the risqué, and the forbidden.

Eventually, around tenth grade, we realized that the library had a higher purpose: Its books were the world we entered as real students in high school, where homework was serious, and grades became important harbingers of our future. So, my friends and I from Central High went to the Parkman Branch with better intentions. (Its rival, the Robin Hood Branch on Seven Mile Road, was the haunt of Mumford High—our rivals and opponents in all endeavors. But in the Parkman Branch, we were certain we even had the best library.) We did some reading in the library, and we shared homework, but we still watched for who was there and with whom. Our hearts fluttered when the current object of our affection came into the reading room. We smuggled in food and soft drinks, and sneaked the occasional cigarette in the men's room, near the stacks, amid whose wisdom of the ages we had indulged some of the urges of early adolescence. It was our place, and we changed its meaning to suit our changing needs.

The school libraries were also important, of course, but in a more maternal way. (In those days, librarians were always women, it seemed.) The school librarian never gave us homework or tests. She welcomed us without any sense of coercion, and she indulged our tastes, letting us wander around and just look—as long as we were quiet. The three schools I attended from kindergarten through twelfth grade were built next to each other and were all constructed similarly. The libraries as I remember them had large windows that looked out on the schools' front lawns. We could sit by the windows and watch the seasons changing, sensing that learning, and reading in particular, was not separate from real life—the way it was in classrooms. The librarian wanted us to find pleasure in her books and to stay quiet. At Roosevelt Elementary (when I was in the third or fourth grade, probably) the librarian invited a few of us to meet with her one day. She asked what kinds of books we liked, and wanted to know if we found them in her library. I was reading boys' baseball books then. I especially liked *The Boy Who Batted 1.000*, and told her so. Some time later, she showed me the new books by that same author that she had bought for the library. I cannot recall having been so indulged in my educational career before—and not much since, as a matter of fact.

Library access at Central High was more structured. Our time there was more often spent on quests assigned by teachers. And even though we learned more there than in most classrooms, we still did not count librarians among those who taught us. We had regular library hours then, and attendance was taken, which meant some among us were not voluntary library users. But we could also use the library during free hours, or after school. Still, it was becoming more of a requirement, and less of a haven, and we found other places to carry out our private business. But the library was still a focus, because it empowered us. It existed only for us, it catered to our needs, it gave us the world and asked nothing in return. The librarian never judged us or gave us assignments or sent nasty notes home to our parents. Misbehavior in the library meant being banned from it, and that was not something most of us wanted. We were indulged there. More than anyplace else in the school, including the lunchroom, it was our place, where we learned how much there was to know, and how to find it on our own. I still recall the comfort of the stacks around me as I poured my broken heart out to Judee one afternoon, touching the books near me as I told her about the treachery of her friend Margie. It was a safe place to be consoled. Even then, in raging youth, we sensed the aura of eternity contained in its wares, a place where private tribulations might be only brief moments.

The library at Wayne State was, in contrast, a necessity. Working my way through undergraduate school meant long hours in the library—weekends, evenings and nights, summers, holidays. If the library didn't have what I needed, I was sunk. Good working relations with the library staff became a primary concern. It was a matter of life and death to convince them that I would bring back a reserve book the very next morning; that it was absolutely imperative to recall a book out on loan because my entire future depended on it; that I would never, never, never again put a book where it didn't belong so it would be there when I needed it, but not for others. It was there that I began to hone political skills of cajoling, and reasoning with the unreasonable, and convincing the powerful to use their power benevolently—skills that I am still trying to perfect. And it was in that library, in a music listening room—which

I entered because the tables and carrels were all taken at mid-term exam time—that I met my first wife. Desperation, triumph, and romance amid the eternal books.

On my last day at Wayne State, the day of my last undergraduate final exam on a halcyon late spring afternoon in 1961, I walked onto the campus and sat under a tree to indulge the moment of release—the pleasure of not having anything to do but work at my paying job at least until the fall. It was the momentary exuberance of having completed the required cycle of my education. The rest was on my own volition. I sat there, drained, but with a nagging sense of something still to be done, until I knew that I first had to say goodbye to the library, to the reserve room, to the librarian on duty that day, to the music listening room on the second floor. And then I was finished with Wayne State.

The library in Ann Arbor was a different story. In part this was because of the sheer size of the University of Michigan as an educational enterprise. In part it was because we were now beginning the 1960s, and before I finished my graduate work the "revolution" would be well under way, and we would reach a new respect for the library as a sanctuary akin to a medieval cathedral. We knew that Jean Jaurès and Mao Tse Tung began their careers as librarians, and that Karl Marx and Vladimir Lenin found a haven in the British Museum Library during their exiles in London. (I managed to visit that shrine in the mid–1960s, and found a security guard who appeared to be as ancient as the precious manuscripts in the rare book collection. I asked if he knew where Marx and Lenin had sat. He pointed to Marx's seat, which was well-known, but for Lenin he was not so certain: "Mr. Lenin spent only a short period here," he said, "and he hasn't been back in a very long time.")

The movement of the sixties brought with it the perception among the university barons that more security was needed, amid the heightening awareness that America's morality was changing. The library acquired uniformed guards and a front gate where our bags were searched as we entered and left. It was they who turned it into a fortress, we reckoned—so during the bad weather months, of which Michigan has an abundance, the library became the obvious best place for a sit-in, next to the president's office. We did serious work there too. To see and be seen in the library was an act of intimidation toward others. With books piled up and pencils chewed to their quicks, with notes being taken furiously, punctuated by long contemplative stares into the middle distance, it was a simple task to make others in your seminar nervous. There was, after all, an assumed quota of "A"s, and small psychological advantages were significant. Even the most honorable and communal of students would be untruthful if they did not admit to this day that the library was one of the more significant battlefronts in the educational wars.

Still, there was time in that library to write existentialist poetry and compose long diatribes against the Establishment. In fact, that's probably why most of those pencils had been worn down to nubbins, and why all those stares into the middle distance led to moments of furious drafting. And there was time, one winter night very late, deep in the bowels of the Michigan library, that my high school friend, now a well-known economist, talked to me about how much he hated medical school and how much he loved the economics courses he'd taken as an undergraduate. Sometime after 2 a.m., my eyes bleary and my strength dissipating, I advised him in classical sixties angst: "To hell with medical school. Do your own thing. And if it doesn't work out, do something else." He did, and every time I disagree when he's quoted in the press, I wonder if I said the right thing.

My first academic job was across the world in Australia, following some time spent in Oxford, and followed by stints in Pakistan and Israel, at universities, and including a kibbutz where I spent a considerable time. The libraries were the touchstones in that uprooted life of more than nine years. The significant difference then was my new status as a faculty member, and one of the few perks distinguishing a fresh junior professor from a doctoral student was in having priority access to the books, and having no late fees imposed. In all of those new cultures the libraries were the universal constants: Dewey-decimaled, with familiar titles, predictable card catalogues, stacks, study carrels, check-out desks, they always offered recognizable ground for an alien academic. Looking back on those constants from the early twenty-first century, I see them as the first buds of globalization, the essential connectors among the growing international community of scholars. And, finally, there was the undiluted chill of pleasure the first time I found my own name in a card catalogue—looking at it for quite a while, and coming back the next day just to look it up again—and finding it in every library I visited. The libraries were immortal, and so would I be—in their card catalogues, in their stacks, and I hoped in their overdue fines paid by those who couldn't bear to part with my book.

I have spent the bulk of my career at Brooklyn College, interrupted by a few years' stint on a congressional staff where the mother of all libraries—the Library of Congress—was at my beck and call. Even though all other library experiences pale before that behemoth of stored knowledge, it is at Brooklyn, more than any other place I've taught at or visited, that the library is the heartbeat of the local life. Our students work long hours at outside jobs to keep body and soul together, and the library is their haven and their sanctuary, and the absolutely necessary gateway to their future. The ebb and flow of students through the library doors reflects the beat of the semester—mid-terms, term paper and final exam time become the rush hours, and the weekends offer some respite, perhaps to catch up on reserve reading. They live overwhelming, convoluted lives, but they seem to find some peace there. At least I hope they do.

I see my student self forty years ago at Wayne State reflected in my twenty-first century students in the library, and find a kind of comfort in realizing how far I've traveled to stay in place. The book I need that is missing from the stacks was, I hope, probably stashed somewhere by a needy undergraduate. I see the students gingerly confronting each other as they stand on their own thresholds of eternity. Even though card catalogues have gone online, and students access the Web at the library computers, the essential library is unchanged. They gather there still for the same reasons as always, and when they leave the college, eventually, many will remember the library more clearly than any other place.

And I hope that some of them say goodbye to the librarians on their last day.

Libraries and Ambivalence

Geraldine DeLuca

Geraldine DeLuca is professor of English at Brooklyn College of the City University of New York. She directs the Freshman English program and has published stories, poems and academic essays.

I

When I go back as far as I can with books, I have a visual memory, like a dark photograph, of myself at the library getting a library card. The building was small, one of a row on a commercial street, and the furniture was dark. But it didn't seem small to me then because I was small too and had nothing to compare it with. I stood against the high counter, reached up and signed my name, and I imagine now that my mother, the librarian and I respected the importance of the moment. I was entering the world of those who read and write, the world of language, as Lacan has it, and though it was women who ushered me in, women who maintained order, it was ultimately the world of the father. I may not have sensed that then: my mother read as well as my father. But as I grew I absorbed the traditional feminine notion that men spoke and wrote and women read and listened. And as the libraries grew larger and more important, more men would be in charge there too.

As a child on that first day in the library, I understood that it was a very serious place. I was now privileged to borrow books, and along with that privilege came responsibility. The books were public property and it was my job as a lender to take care of them. I ran my hands over the covers and pages. This was what it looked like and smelled like and felt like to read: To be in this place with its wooden tables, its black linoleum countertop, its walls lined with books. To choose a book from the shelf. To open to its black letters with

70

broken serifs on grainy, eggshell paper. To find a story about a child, and maybe next to it an illustration, a wobbly line drawing of a girl, or sometimes even a painted inset with a line from the text quoted at the bottom of the page.

This was the gift and burden of civilization. I could read these books; I could lose myself in their stories and images. And they would civilize me. (Or, sometimes, as Mark Twain put it, "sivilize" me.) I would absorb their messages just as I absorbed my Aunt Mary's interest in how clean I was. "Did you wash behind your ears?" she would ask, because that's what one was supposed to ask children, and I would say yes, but I would worry. Had I? What did it say about me if I hadn't? The library, of course, could also liberate me from such questions. It could explain to me why my Aunt Mary persisted in asking them, and I could take an oppositional or at least more distanced stance in relation to people like her. I could become less parochial. Like Huck, at least in my own imagination, I could light out for the territories. That too was what it meant to be civilized.

I love and depend on libraries every day of my life. As I write, the Brooklyn College Library is under major renovation, and I feel keenly the loss of easy access to its books. That access is a privilege I have taken for granted during the twenty-seven years I have been teaching there. It cannot be replaced by Barnes and Noble, despite its comfortable chairs and cappuccino bars. It doesn't help to have Amazon.com. For one thing, their books are not free. For another, there are no journals, no microfilms, no archives, no university press titles, no pamphlets, no documents, no special collections. There is only what the market will bear, only what is current. In the library—even the not-so-vast version of the Brooklyn College library that existed before the doors closed—I sat in the midst of the house of knowledge.

What I am exploring here, then, is not the value of libraries, but the symbolic weight of them in my own life—as a woman and as an academic. I am writing about how they have functioned as a defining force in my life. There has never been a time when libraries have not mattered to me. When I told a colleague that I was thinking about writing an essay called "libraries and ambivalence," she said immediately, "Yes, I know what you mean. Write it." It's a feeling many of us seem to carry with us. The library is our second home, our alma mater. It makes demands on us. It has expectations. It defines us as people who read and write, and thus is a powerful reflecter of our desires and our fears.

II

A few years after I got my library card at the 18th Avenue storefront in Brooklyn, a new, more official building opened a few blocks away. It was a free-standing grey stone structure with two floors. The first was for adults, the second for children. Sometimes there were story hours, but I was a little too old to give myself up to them. I sensed something both too stern and too precious about the librarians who read those stories, and I steered clear of that special room where the others—the good children—went to listen in rapt attention. What I looked for as the years passed were novels, and I can still remember where certain authors were located: Louisa May Alcott, Elizabeth Enright, Beverly Cleary, Sydney Taylor. Every morning, I turned on the yellow lamp over my bed and read about those heroines in their mostly safe domestic spaces, working out their dilemmas in two hundred pages, and I was completely happy. Like the girls in those stories, my life was sheltered and circumscribed by rules that I mostly obeyed, and I didn't ask for anything more risk-taking than they offered.

Those books were as much a part of my childhood experience as the actual people and places in my life, and I have from time to time gone back to take a second look at them. Sometimes it was by way of reading the books to my children. At other times, I read them by myself. For a long time, I taught a course in children's literature, and I would go to the second floor of the Donnell Library in Manhattan to find copies of those books I loved so many years ago—not the *Alice* books or *Winnie-the-Pooh* or *Charlotte's Web*, but the others that no one writes about or reprints anymore. Sometimes I found them and sometimes I didn't. One of my favorite books during that long stretch of childhood that used to be called the dormant period was Elizabeth Enright's *The Four-Story Mistake*. I remember the heroine's fascination with the cupola in her odd new house. I was captivated by the image of enclosure in a high place with space to dream and windows to look out of. It is like the library itself, or like the ivory tower of the university perhaps. But also, more primally for me, it was an archetypal female space—Rapunzel's prison, or the house in the forest where the fairy tale heroine watched for the coming of her prince. It was the place where the young woman waited for her life to start. It was also the retreat she returned to—once her adult life of caring for others took her over—in order to find herself again. I am still happy to withdraw each morning to my small study on the third story of my house, to look out my window at the limbs of the maple tree in the backyard and at the roof top of the grey house across the way.

Those habits of mind began early and stayed with me. They are the habits of a reader and a writer, and no doubt Enright was able to describe that space so lovingly because she was a writer herself. And she was a writer who needed to recreate the comforts of those books, with their sense of order and certainty, their simple clarities about what children needed, and their avoidance of the darker side of life. *The Four-Story Mistake* was published in 1942, which makes me wonder if the book was not Enright's retreat from the war itself.

Thinking about these comforting texts now, I wonder about the books I didn't want to read. They were even approved books, classics, smart kids read them. *Tom Sawyer*, *Huckleberry Finn*, *David Copperfield*. It wasn't until I was an undergraduate that I read any of them. I remember sitting on my bed, at about age 11, trying to find my way into them and not succeeding. Tom's pranks were too distant, too boyish, Dickens's baroque world was too sinister and full of exaggeration, and I wanted more female characters. Sinister fathers, dark rages, children being beaten by cruel schoolmasters—they had nothing to do with me: with my housebound mother who drove my father to work every morning, who cleaned the house each day, who had a perfect dinner on the table every night at six o'clock, who read *The New York World Telegram and Sun* in the afternoon and novels at night; or with my responsible, good, intelligent father who read *The New York Times* and Bertrand Russell; or with our clean house; or with my clean self. Nothing like Dickens happened in our family. I didn't want to know. So I put them aside. But at the same time I sensed that there was something wrong with me for not liking them.

And of course, the reading list for anybody's life is too long. The tension between what I should have been reading, should have been facing, should have been current about, should still be current about, and what I actually know and get pleasure from reading is still there. Awareness came slowly for me and there are always new books, and time slips away. But maybe now, sometimes, I read for different reasons: not to be lulled, soothed into my position, but to understand what's really going on, why there's so much violence and grief in life, and to try to do something about it in my small way, as a teacher, and to take some unguilty pleasure in my own existence whenever I can get it.

III

I remember a few years ago reading Terry Eagleton on Freud and being struck for the first time by the power of Freud's "death wish." "The final goal of life," Eagleton writes, "is death, a return to that blissful inanimate state where the ego cannot be injured."

> …The ego is a pitiable, precarious entity, battered by the external world, scourged by the cruel upbraidings of the superego, plagued by the greedy, insatiable demands of the id. Freud's compassion for the ego is a compassion for the human race, labouring under the almost intolerable demands placed upon it by a civilization built upon the repression of desire and the deferment of gratification [161].

The child entering the world of language, Lacan says, enters a world of loss where the words never compensate for the wordless paradise they supposedly replace.

> In Lacanian theory, it is an original lost object—the mother's body—
> which drives forward the narrative of our lives.... Something must be
> lost or absent in any narrative for it to unfold: if everything stayed in
> place there would be no story to tell. This loss is distressing, but excit-
> ing as well: desire is stimulated by what we cannot possess, and this
> is one source of narrative satisfaction [Eagleton, 186].

So as we enter the world of language, the world of others where we are no
longer at the center, we find parallel stories to read and tell, to heal from
inevitable wounds. For me, the library is the site of this struggle, this tension,
where one learns to make other arrangements to compensate for the old ones
that growing up has destroyed. It is the place where one works hard and chan-
nels one's sexual energy into achievement, where one finds the pleasures that
such work brings, and where one thus shores oneself up against the fear and
seductive call of death.

In *Hunger of Memory*, Richard Rodriguez dramatizes this movement in
his chronicle of growing up in Southern California and moving away from the
Mexican heritage of his parents. He gives up Spanish, the soothing words of
home, for the language of school. And the older he gets, the more fiercely he
embraces the world of books to shore up an identity. In his chapter "The
Achievement of Desire," he describes himself as a graduate student—one who
has finally "arrived" in the mainstream culture—writing a dissertation on
Shakespeare at the British Museum. He has become a superior student, a master of English. His subject, one could say inevitably, is pastoral: the cultured
man's lament for the lost world of innocence.

> After only two or three months in the reading room of the British
> Museum, it became clear that I had joined a lonely community. Around
> me each day were dour faces eclipsed by large piles of books. There
> were the regulars ... and there was the historian who chattered madly
> to herself. ("Oh dear! Oh! Now, what's this? What? Oh, my!") There
> were also the faces of young men and women worn by long study. And
> everywhere eyes turned away the moment our glance accidentally met.
> Some person I sat beside day after day, yet we passed silently at the
> end of the day, strangers. Still, we were united by a common respect
> for the written word and for scholarship. We did form a union, though
> one in which we remained distant from one another [69 –70].

He felt a bond also with the writers whose books he read, but thought about
how specialized and esoteric those books were. He wondered if his dissertation was "an act of social withdrawal": "Who, beside my dissertation director
and a few faculty members, would ever read what I wrote?" (70).

Hunger of Memory, in fact, belies these concerns. In choosing the sustained loneliness necessary to write it, Rodriguez has made himself famous in
a way, a conservative voice in the debate about affirmative action, but also a

person pushing against the archetypal story of the immigrant child who makes good, articulating a particularly elegiac and to me comforting reflection on the gains and losses of a bookish life. This is what it feels like to be a person who spends long hours alone with books, who establishes a competitive stance in relation to them, who sees them as the standard, the sustenance, and also the thing to be overthrown.

IV

I too pursued the world of books until one day I found myself in graduate school at New York University, not quite sure what I was doing there. It was as if I had drifted downriver on a log. One day I was reading novels under my yellow lamp, the next I was reading the complete works of John Donne in one week. Or not reading them. Pretending to read them. Morning, noon, and night. And that was just one of four courses. They all required formal research papers. I remember one graduate professor's comment on a paper I did on "The Goddess Fortuna in 'The Posies' of George Gascoigne" that I made Gascoigne sound very dull. And Gascoigne *was* dull to me. Why was I interested in the Goddess Fortuna, Lady Luck, the woodcut image of a man bound to a wheel? Maybe I felt some kinship to that creature with his arms and legs stretched out, subject to life's contingencies, not exactly on a wheel of fire, but feeling upside down. I never allowed myself to explore. I never connected the reading to myself because that's not what graduate students were supposed to do. I just found all the references and laid them out. I was imitating what I thought to be the work of a scholar: counting images. Whatever naïve sense of freedom I had had as a writer in high school had been slowly filtered out in college. By graduate school I was selfless, having achieved a kind of tormented acolyte perfection in which I knew that any false move could lead to humiliation by way of a withering comment on a paper, and that my mission was to make sure nobody found out how unworthy I was.

That is the dominant memory I have of graduate school. Of being a fraud. I'm sure now, that that is one of the purposes of graduate school—to make us feel fraudulent. It is a universe built on public postures and a standard of excellence that only a rarefied few can achieve. Many, like Mr. Ramsay in *To the Lighthouse*, probably suffer from the narrow recognition that they will never live up to the extraordinary standards they set for themselves, but they can't imagine another way to be. In *The Drama of the Gifted Child*, Alice Miller writes of the "false self" that many children construct to please unresponsive parents. To be who one really is, if one could ever find it, could not be good enough. One has to learn what the parent finds acceptable and be that, often at great cost to the self. Only then does one get to feel a kind of approval that passes for love. But then, in response to one's assumption of a fraudulent self, one may become grandiose or depressed.

For me, graduate school reproduced these conditions. Day after day I went to the library to work on my dissertation. And now, replacing the humble two-story structure in Brooklyn, there stood the grand and imposing Elmer Holmes Bobst Library that blocked out the sun of Washington Square. I remember being struck by the hubris of its huge atrium, the great walled-in empty space. I stood on the higher balconies and looked down at the marble floor with its dizzying design, and I was intimidated. I sat in the library and watched people: people reading, people writing, people sleeping, people scratching their heads, people going to the bathroom every ten minutes for a cigarette. It seemed to me that I wasted a lot of time trying to get comfortable—finding a place with enough light, a good chair, organizing myself, copying long passages out of journals, getting the citations right.

There was one graduate professor, though, whom I remember fondly, who taught medieval literature. She was also the only woman on the graduate faculty. Something in me leaned toward Sir Gawain and King Arthur and Chaucer, "the lyf so short, the craft so long to lerne"—that line from Chaucer's *Parliament of Fowls,* pronounced fools. Translating the Middle English in the margins was like learning an easy foreign language, becoming privy to the in-jokes and satirical thrusts and linguistic grace notes that were known to Chaucer's audience. I learned to love the ornate romances which affirmed an elegance, a humility, and a God-centered order in the universe, and I read in contented obedience. In a way the experience mirrored the security of reading those girlhood novels.

The female professor used to tell amiable anecdotes about her adventures with books: that, for example, she needed different eyeglasses for different texts. I loved that homely detail. I also remember her saying that she had spent her "salad days" in the New York Public Library, and that depressed me. I wasn't even sure what she meant at first. Then I looked up the phrase in Bartlett's and discovered that it was from *Antony and Cleopatra.* Cleopatra speaks of her salad days when she was green in judgment. So that's what she did with her youth: the same thing I was doing with mine. Only she didn't seem depressed about it, which depressed me even more.

Perhaps the most endearing detail about this professor for me was that, like me, she spoke with a New York accent. That she was a woman and that she pronounced words the way I did might have cheered me, but at the time I was still too frightened to use those facts to help myself. What I needed then was someone to give me permission to write something more connected to my own interests than the dry research papers I regularly turned out. My medieval literature professor, kind as she was, could not help me out of the psychic prison where I lived during that period. But many other writers—Adrienne

Rich, Nancy Mairs, Peter Elbow, Natalie Goldberg, Geoff Dyer, bell hooks, Jane Tompkins, Mike Rose, to name just a few—would become models of freedom in the years to come.

And the library stood there, waiting, as it were, for me to be ready for it, to figure out all it had to give me, to mine that small piece of its offerings that I was ready to find. T. S. Eliot writes that "the end of all our exploring/ Will be to arrive where we started/ And know the place for the first time" (145). The library holds nearly everything. It represents energy and creativity, freedom of thought and speech, the careful quest to understand and to share one's understanding. It represents also the alluring, elusive prize of recognition. A spot on a library shelf is the "achievement of desire," as Rodriguez would put it, the momentary triumph over our own death. The library also represents the likely fall into forgetfulness and physical decay of those texts that do not survive the first or second printing. And by their absence, it represents all the works that don't get published because they aren't considered fashionable or erudite or marketable enough and all the works that never get written because their would-be authors never learn to read, are never encouraged to pay attention to their thoughts, never overcome the injunction to be silent.

I am a middle-aged woman in the library, and I experience it still as a physical place. I crouch along the bottom shelves looking for books. Each one is a gift and a promise. I sit in a wooden chair, my back against the slats, the dust in my nose, noticing the smell of books, the weight of them in my arms as I check them out. And now that I am a bit freer than I was in graduate school, now that my choices are more considerate of my own real interests, I am happier there.

During the past two summers I spent five weeks in London teaching Shakespeare and creative writing in Brooklyn College's Summer in London Program. Both times, I lived five minutes away from the new British Library on Euston Road. It now houses the book collection that used to be in the British Museum. The old reading room was famous for its grandeur and for the many eminent figures who worked there. When I ask people who remember it what it was like, they say, "Now that was a place." I arrived years too late to use it, but I can respond that this too is a place worth being. The street is always busy, and the air smells of auto exhausts. But the building itself is set back from the street and when one passes through the outer gates into the outdoor plaza, one enters a space of calm and grace. The building is red brick with red and aqua trim. It has terraced, sloping roofs, smooth walls and sleek lines—a beautiful anomaly among the strange and ugly glass structures that characterize much of modern London architecture.

The first time I went there I applied for an application to use the collections. Because I had a faculty card from Brooklyn College, I was automatically eligible. I planned to use it often to call up books on Shakespeare, but most days I was too busy teaching or reading student papers or seeing plays or compulsively wandering the streets like the tourist that I was. Every so often, however, particularly when I was feeling lonely, three thousand miles from home, I would go to the humanities collection and just sit there. And when I did, I felt that I was among kindred spirits. I was, if not a citizen of the world, a citizen of libraries. I was surrounded by people like myself who reverenced books, who did their work carefully and quietly. They came in the morning with their laptops and they left at night. They had lunch in the quiet café downstairs. Sometimes I would look for a book just to see if it was there. If it wasn't in one collection, I'd look in another. When I found it, I was happy. I could read it or not, but it was there. And the people beside me were writing their own new books—or I imagined that they were—and others were working carefully to make sure that books were accessible. It all seemed like a labor of love and faith, the mark of a great civilization.

In the outdoor plaza is a monumental statue of Sir Isaac Newton leaning over to measure the world with his compass. The statue is modeled on a famous drawing by the romantic poet William Blake, and the first time I saw it, I was startled that the sculptor would choose an image charged with such dark associations. Newton was a troublesome figure for Blake, one whose science and Deism deromanticized the rich spiritual and imaginative universe that Blake inhabited. In *Europe*, Blake writes:

> A mighty Spirit leap'd from the land of Albion,
> Nam'd Newton: he seiz'd the trump & blow'd the enormous blast!
> Yellow as leaves of autumn, the myriads of Angelic hosts
> Fell thro' the wintry skies, seeking their graves,
> Rattling their hollow bones in howling and lamentation [quoted in Bloom, 170].

Harold Bloom comments: "When Newton blows the trump, that is, explains the universe, the Angelic hosts are revealed as dying leaves, as creatures with hollow bones overready for their graves.... Newton's discoveries at once testify to the grandeur of Urizen ["reason" or "your reason"?] as Nature's god, and are a final kind of naturalistic reductiveness, since they demonstrate to Blake how remote nature really is from Blake's ideal human" (171). How strange then that this ambiguous image would appear here. And yet it is also fitting, for it embodies the intellectual and emotional struggles the library houses, the gains and the losses that attend our quest for knowledge, achievement and technological advancement. It reminds us, as we lean over our work, singlemindedly pursuing our next goal, what richness and comfort we may leave behind.

Works Cited

Bloom, Harold. *Blake's Apocalypse: A Study in Poetic Argument.* Garden City, NY: Anchor, 1965.

Eagleton, Terry. *Literary Theory: An Introduction.* Minneapolis: University of Minnesota Press, 1983.

Eliot, T. S. "Little Gidding." *The Complete Poems and Plays, 1909–1950.* New York: Harcourt, Brace & World, 1962.

Enright, Elizabeth. *The Four-Story Mistake.* Henry Holt, 1942; rpt. New York: Puffin, 1997.

Johnson, Alexandra. *The Hidden Writer: Diaries and the Creative Life.* New York: Doubleday, 1997.

Miller, Alice. *The Drama of the Gifted Child: The Search for the True Self.* New York: Basic Books, 1997.

Rodriguez, Richard. *Hunger of Memory: The Education of Richard Rodriguez.* New York: Bantam, 1982.

It Was Something Like This, I Think

Don Reich

Don Reich taught and administered at Oberlin College and Brooklyn College. He leads the Canal Street Jazz Band on Friday nights at the Cajun Restaurant (no cover, no minimum), Eighth Avenue at 16th Street, in New York City.

"Libraries?" she said. "You must have been in hundreds." A friendly exaggeration, of course, but what followed, in the seconds before my reply, was an unmediated flashback. Not to one of the elaborate research libraries I'd used. And not to one of the reading-room libraries where so much intellectually relaxed undergraduate and postgraduate studying was done. I flashed back instead to two book-filled spaces in Two Rivers, Wisconsin, a fishing, farming, and factory town of ten thousand souls built on a spit of sand that eases about four miles out into Lake Michigan ... same longitude, more or less, as Milwaukee ... same latitude, more or less, as Green Bay.

St. Luke's

The first flashback was to St. Luke's, a Roman Catholic school, K through 8, as they now say, kindergarten up to high school, as they said then, and to Sister Constantcia. She was a tall, well built, imperious figure who usually taught one of the two eighth grades. No martinet, but her bearing, stature, and voice earned respect from almost every one of us. She had another side though, and that's what brought me to a room on the second floor at St. Luke's, to Leonardo and Christ, and to a solitude in the midst of clamor that made me think I was someone special.

80

Recently, on a nostalgia trip, I went back to the school. It stands empty, a basement and two stories high. Across the street on one side is what used to be the town vocational school and on another side is the office building of the Hamilton Manufacturing Company, where at first the fathers and later the mothers as well of most of the students worked on production lines that turned out drafting tables, printers' equipment, furniture for doctors' examining rooms and dentists' offices, laboratory equipment for schools and colleges, and eventually even clothes dryers.

There have been no students at St. Luke's for several years now, and it soon will move dramatically from one end of the generational chain to the other as it shares the ambiguous fate of many schools in the old part of towns by being recycled into a residence for seniors. I truly felt myself in a time warp: as if to mock the passage of more than fifty years the interior was virtually the same as I remembered.

I started with the basement: the gym, as dreary as ever, a basket at each end but too narrow and too short to have out-of-bounds lines and too low to permit a good two-handed set shot from beyond the free-throw circle. The framed doors leading into the classroom hallway on the first floor seemed familiar. The communal closets that ran along each wall in the corridor, where students hung coats and left galoshes, were absolutely familiar. The closet doors, the very same dark wood doors, didn't hang from hinges as modern lockers do but rotated on steel poles that ran from the floor to the top of each closet. I tried a door; it seemed sturdy enough to go at least another fifty.

St. Luke's had no library and I don't remember its having a principal either. But up there on the second floor, diagonally across from my classroom, was a somewhat mysterious place with a door unlike those on the classrooms. It was never fully open. On the few occasions when it was ajar you could see a large wooden desk in the center of what seemed to be a high, narrow room. We may even have called it the principal's office, but for me it was about books.

Books had to do with school. My family was not one of those fairy-tale outfits where there was reading before bed every night and age-appropriate storybooks lying around the house. My mother had gone to school out in the country through the fourth grade; I knew she could read although I almost never saw her reading. And my father was heavily into work. He went to work at seven o'clock, walked home from work at noon for what we called dinner, went back to work at one o'clock, and walked home quickly at five o'clock for supper and to get the other work done, the work around the house and the work in the garden or the work on the car. When the work was done he read the paper and listened to the radio. From him I got a tremendous work ethic and a daily-news ethic, but no reading ethic.

I did read quickly but I didn't go out of my way to bring home anything other than schoolbooks. Instead, I devoted myself to becoming a great athlete and a great musician. Books probably came in fourth or fifth, behind radio and hanging out at Connie Althen's, an empty lot just around the corner named after its absentee owner. ("Where you goin' after supper?" "Connie Althen's.")

I was a pretty good student. Not that I set out to be such, but studious seemed like an appropriate way to be in school, and, besides, I found most of the textbooks quite interesting, a window on the outside world that was not otherwise available in Two Rivers, Wisconsin. There was no bookstore. The local newspaper was very local and the *Milwaukee Journal*, a first-rate newspaper, came into our house only on Sunday mornings.

Studiousness earned me a privilege now and then and one of them got me into that mysterious room at St. Luke's. It was a day when we had a longish reading assignment, in geography, my favorite subject, to be done in about 45 minutes. I must have read the material beforehand or been familiar with it because after a few minutes I sat back at my desk as if to announce that I was finished. (I had done this before; maybe often.)

Sister Constantcia noticed that I had stopped reading and motioned to me to step into the hall. She said nothing but led me across the hall, opened the door of that special room and said, "You'll find something to read here." She told me to remain until she came back for me and closed the door as she left. (That's one way of knowing when you're in a library: someone says, "You'll find something to read here.")

What a moment! The room wasn't large but it seemed to be crammed on three walls, almost floor to ceiling, with books. Years later, I first saw Carl Spitzweg's humorous painting, "Der Bucherwurm." A tall man in a frock coat and leather boots stands precariously on the very top of a library ladder in the "Metaphysik" section of a tall room stuffed with books, holding one closed book between his legs, another under his left arm, an open one in his right hand, and reading from another in his left hand, a shaft of light from overhead throwing his shadow down the shelves in front of him. When I saw it my instant reference was to that moment at St. Luke's: a tall room, full of books.

In a strange library, as we know, the right book falls off the shelf into our hands. I don't recall what attracted my eye, but my hand reached for a slightly oversize volume. It was an illustrated work on the drawings and scientific writing of Leonardo da Vinci. The flying machine was there and some especially intriguing details of relationships between gears and cams. Thus began a feeling that grew over time that there was a special relationship between Leonardo and me. That is, I have never failed, no matter what the place or time, to attend to anything about him that crosses my vision or hearing.

Not long after, it happened again: another reading assignment finished quickly and another invitation to find "something to read" in that room. I thought briefly about going back to Leonardo but, wondering if I would ever be in the room again, chose to see what else there was. This time it was a more portentous-looking volume, a life of Christ. It's not that I was particularly religious. I wasn't, although there were those occasional times, probably on a gloomy day in Lent, the statuary in the church shrouded, incense having been dispersed, and we kneeling or sitting in candlelight, that I wondered what to call the power of the moment that I seemed to sense.

Whose life of Christ was it? Perhaps it was the translation of Lebreton. His work, I understand, was favored by Roman Catholic teachers. In any case, it was heavy going. There were no beautiful drawings of outrageous mechanical ideas, the type face was over-elaborate, and the book simply didn't have the power of the Leonardo. Nonetheless, some kind of mnemonic must be at work because each year around Easter when I look for the listing by public television of its four-hour special on the early Christian sects I think back to that life of Christ and that room.

On my nostalgia trip I spoke with a couple of classmates from St. Luke's and asked them about that room on the second floor. "Oh, you mean the principal's office?" they said. I was sorry to hear that response. I wanted one, at least, to mention books. None did.

Was I the only St. Luke's student ever to use that library? What about the nuns? I'm left with the very strong impression that something made a very strong impression on me but on no one else. I must have been impressionistic. As for my classmates, my retrospective hunch is that the readers among them didn't need to discover a library at St. Luke's because they had long since discovered another one, one that my overwhelming commitment of time and energy to athletics and music had kept me out of.

Joseph Mann

After whom, other than Andrew Carnegie, are small-town libraries in the Midwest named? Well, Joseph Mann, for one. Joseph came relatively early to Two Rivers. He and brothers Leopold and Henry left the urbanities of Milwaukee around 1860 to make their fortunes "up north." When you live in the midst of a forest you make use of the wood, so they manufactured chairs, pails, and tubs. They soon practically owned the town and in the 1890s the family began to return some of their fortune to it. There had been a couple of earlier attempts at libraries, such as a reading room sponsored by the Temple of Honor, a temperance organization. The reading-room plan failed and, as I could testify growing up there decades later, so did the temperance plan.

Temperance may have failed but Chatauqua didn't (thereby probably showing once again the superior power of good talk over sumptuary ideology). The weekly meetings of the Reading Circle, sponsored by the Chatauqua movement, were "very serious and high-minded" and sometimes included music. From the members' need for a wider selection of books and a better place to meet, a library emerged. Joseph Mann's widow offered $1,000 if the building would be named after her husband. Her money and that of other donors got the building up and furniture in it. There was nothing left for books so the library association mortgaged the real estate at $500 to start the collection.

The collection and the readership grew so well that soon a new building was needed. The association apparently decided that even if you have had a good Mann you don't necessarily have to keep a wealthy Carnegie down. They wrote Andrew Carnegie's secretary, telling him they needed $20,000 and adding, "if you cannot get $20,000 for us, $15,000 will do nicely." Carnegie sent $12,500, but Mann's name remained on the building.

I don't remember my first visit to this building but I do remember that it felt different from all the other public buildings in town. It was partly the building's design itself. The local committee hoped for a "classic" structure. But the Wisconsin Free Library Commission disliked "classic" and found a draftsman in Madison, the state capital, who would propose something quite different. For a town far in the upper Midwest he offered a mission-style building, 60' by 34', in a light buff brick with green tile roof and white stone trim. There were two stories: a main floor, reached directly by a few steps up from the street, and a high basement under it.

Once inside the entry you climbed a wide wooden staircase that seemed sway-backed, as if, by my time, weary with the tread of so many, many readers. At the top, a wide entryway and just beyond it, dead center and maybe only five steps away, the check-out desk. I always felt I should check *in*, as if, having entered this unusual place, I should present myself and say, "I'm here, I'm going to look at some books, and I may even take one home with me." An announcement, that is, which I half expected someone to acknowledge with something like, "Welcome! Congratulations! You are a *good* person!"

For a blue-collar kid it was something like a special entrance, not grand exactly, but certainly not ordinary. From sidewalk level, leaving behind the block-long, four story, red-brick aluminum-kitchen-utensil factory just across the street, into the entryway and then up the wide steps to a sotto-voce world of browns and tans, sturdy tables, chairs, and shelves.

A short architectural digression. After some years more space was needed at Joseph Mann. Carnegie no longer was in the library-building business so a new building was out of the question. Instead Joseph Mann was added onto. Adding onto existing public buildings, as everyone knows, is one of the most dangerous activities practiced in the Western World, generally to be regarded as a form of institutionally-practiced vandalism.

So it was with Joseph Mann. They added a piece on the back and another on the side. They took my entrance away from the center front and put it around the corner, on the side. I continued to visit Joseph Mann on visits "home" but felt specifically resentful of the changes and usually spent only ten or fifteen uncomfortable minutes not finding what I came for. The power of an original association between a physical setting and a good intellectual experience is about as strong as power—of any kind—gets.

Last month I drove down the main street and came to the intersection from which, looking downhill on 15th Street, you can see Joseph Mann. I saw only a 60' by 34' mission-style building of light buff brick with white stone trim—and nothing added on.

It was an illusion, of course, but a good one. Less pleasant was a screaming sign on the side facing up toward the main street, with letters as tall as the windows: FOR LEASE. Joseph Mann's writ had run out. There is a fine new library a few blocks away, in a city park that looks across the road to Lake Michigan. It's called the Lester Library. Another millennium, another benefactor. I use it and enjoy it on every visit (and they're getting oftener). But I still look for library buildings whose entrance is dead center, street level, with a wide staircase. If there's a factory across the street, whether making aluminum pots and pans or tenured faculty members, that's okay with me.

But back to my earlier visits to Joseph Mann. Once I got beyond the naïve feeling that I had to check in whenever I reached the top of the staircase I always turned left immediately, stopping briefly at a round oak table where the new books were laid out flat. The fiction I glanced at, just in case it had something to do with music. Non-fiction was another matter. I handled each book, scanning the table of contents and sometimes reading a random paragraph.

And that, as they say, is how I came to have another lifelong association, this time not with a figure, Leonardo, but with an event. The book was graphically and physically oversized. Once I got beyond the incredible photo on the jacket it became emotionally oversized as well. I was astounded by what I saw on page after page after page. It was a collection of Mathew B. Brady's battlefield photographs from the American Civil War. I stood with it a moment, then took it to a table and sat with it, and then stayed with it a long time.

The extraordinary clarity of Brady's photography combined with its subject matter—mostly horrendous panoramic scenes of twisted, dead forms—men, horses, trees—incongruously across the page from live encampments and fully transparent portraits of officers—had its impact. It exploded the notion that I could get everything I needed from a good text; it compelled me to become not only a reader but a viewer as well. And it brought all five senses to the understanding of something that until then had been merely history. I believe that every photograph that I have seen since of a dramatic American event has been filtered through that first experience with Brady's pictures.

You were a reader when you walked up the steps of Joseph Mann, and you could become a viewer in a revelatory instant, as I think I did. But you couldn't yet be a listener there, no matter how inspiring the visit. There were a few shelves on music and musicians, but recordings were not yet part of the collection.

Too bad, because my strong interest in athletics had begun to wane and my interest in music was growing. The athletic coaches had not invited me to the starting five or starting eleven, or starting any-other-number, but the band director had given me a first chair in the trumpet section. Long hours of practice flew by as I established an embouchure and technique. Soon I gathered the best players out of the school band to play, at first for fun and later for pride and money *and* fun, the Bohemian (Czech) folk music that I heard every day, at home, at dances, picnics and parades, on local radio, on recordings, everywhere. One thing led to another: an old-time band, as the Bohemian bands were called, then a dance band, the "serious" repertoire of the school band, solos and ensembles at festivals and competitions, and I began to think *career*.

There came a time, then, when I did my left turn at the top of the staircase but breezed by the new-books table. I was purposeful, on a mission: to find out what those several shelves on music had to offer. My approach was going to be comprehensive. I would scan all the titles, then go back to the most arresting, skim it, then go to the next most interesting, skim it, and so on. It didn't happen. I don't remember where on the shelves I found *Shining Trumpets*, bound in purple with the title in gold, but my scanning stopped there. And I didn't skim. I read, hard.

I had been staying up late on weekend nights, waiting for AM radio reception to clear so I could pick up live remote broadcasts from Chicago. They broadcast regularly from the Aragon and Trianon Ballrooms, two dance halls on the north and south sides of the city. The ballrooms featured dance orchestras common to the Big Band era, but sweet bands rather than hot bands. I liked the sounds, especially the ensemble playing in the brasses and reeds, but what I particularly waited for was the occasional hot interlude by a smaller band-within-the-band made up of the rhythm section and three horns—trumpet, clarinet, and trombone. Now and then I also found live broadcasts of pure Dixieland groups on national networks originating in New York or New Orleans.

It was the clarity and polyphony of small-group jazz that grabbed my ear. I knew the sounds well and even knew some of the players. But I had no musical or cultural context for what I wanted to hear and, most of all, to play myself. In *Shining Trumpets*, a history of jazz, Rudi Blesh provided the context. It was all there: where and how it started, how it moved up the river from New Orleans and into the "territories" before going to Chicago and New York; why the instrumentation was what it was, who the big names were, what the best recordings were. I luxuriated in the story.

My career went in a different direction. But I've never stopped playing the trumpet—except, dammit, in graduate school!—and I've told the story over and over again, more often than any story I know. I tell it to myself and to many others, sometimes speaking it, sometimes playing it. Blesh's history came to be regarded as a "popular" account, not good enough for the heavy-browed critics who tried to cerebralize jazz. It used to be a music that had to be danced to, or at least moved to; it became in part an art form that requires reverence, in a niche so narrow that there isn't even room enough to move.

Shining Trumpets isn't in the Joseph Mann–cum–Lester Library collection today and neither are Brady's photographs. I hope they were borrowed until they fell apart, but I doubt it. A classmate recently told me she may have seen the book of Leonardo's drawings from St. Luke's while browsing at the Two Rivers Historical Society. The others may be there, too. The historical societies of many towns, along with the "collectibles" shops in abandoned main-street storefronts may well be the "library that used to be" for their communities.

A Temporary Building

"There's nothing as permanent as a T building." I heard that bit of student irony within days of beginning my first semester at the University of Wisconsin, and it was still in use when I left with an A.B. The G.I. Bill produced a student body in the '40s and '50s that overwhelmed most public universities. They reacted with a building boom of temporary structures until they could find out what size they would be once the bulge of veterans had passed. T-16 at Madison, for example, was a large, low, rectangular space that every semester held the 700 students enrolled in Professor William Stokes's lectures in Political Science 101. T-16 was no fun even though Stokes was pretty funny. I could hear him, as amplified, but I could hardly see him. But it and all the other "Ts" stayed long after the vets were gone.

Another T building, different size, different shape, houses my best bookplace memories from that time. The main library, a prepossessing classic stone structure that also housed the state historical society, wasn't ready for the vets either, particularly for the numbers that would need reading-room space. So the university took double advantage of its deficiency; first, by accepting the federal government's offer of two very long, very large Quonset huts, and second, by placing them, end to end, on a pleasant quadrangle just behind the main library.

Now that doesn't sound pretty, and at first sight the corrugated metal in particular made the two long Quonsets seem like very illegitimate offspring of their steady old classical parent next door. On the other hand, their roof line, a perfect half circle, ground to ground, was so much more welcoming than the lying-on-its-back cereal box of T-16 that there was no contest.

What settled the matter was not form but content. Professor Stokes's lectures in T-16 introduced me to the field of study that became my own, but the heavy stuff to be found in the Quonsets was of another magnitude. It was heavy in the sense that it was difficult, somewhat esoteric, and, to my taste, fascinating. I'm talking here not about the *required* readings—they were okay—but about the *recommended* readings.

The huts lay flat on the ground, no special entrance, just a couple of aluminum swinging doors with a windbreak against the Wisconsin winter. But it was warm inside and the reserved material was right there. The image of a cafeteria comes to mind: I was, in fact, hungry for the readings and I was glad to have them quickly. It was instant, and it was gratification.

Like most cafeterias this one had busy and less busy times. Saturday afternoons, I found, offered a sweet combination: the fewest readers, the least distraction and, on my part, the most relaxed time of the week to deal with what seemed so much more interesting than ordinary textbook content. I think, for example, of a number of pieces by an eminent sociologist of the time, Howard Becker. His writing was speculative, dense, and theoretical; he seemed always to be working out on the edge of conventional discourse and content. I knew I wouldn't be held responsible for what Becker said, but I didn't really care. My reading was almost recreational, as if wandering around in his speculative and unconventional places was a luxury.

I never gave a thought to majoring in sociology. Exciting, yes, but somehow too soft, too far from the harder, more hierarchical stuff that I found in studying the institutions of politics and government. Political science claimed then, as it still does, to be the true study of power, a concept and phenomenon that I seemed to need, for reasons still not clear—aside from being an Aries—to contend with.

Howard Becker, I will add, was a member of the Wisconsin faculty. I didn't take his courses, but I did, in my last year at Madison, get to know him slightly. I volunteered, as he did, to join a faculty-student luncheon group, part of the university's effort at reducing the awesome distance between well-known lecturers and undergraduates. His appearance and manner confirmed my impression of a man who thought and wrote as he did: bushy-browed, craggy-faced, rather thick eyeglasses, serious, intense, questioning, forthright, giving of himself in the interest of his work and his community. We met for lunch only a few times but it was enough to bring a pleasant kind of closure, an additional reward as it were, for those Saturday afternoon hours in the Quonsets.

Reading Room Redux

My preference for reading rooms over the *Big Library* continued in graduate school. Widener stands majestically near the center of the Harvard Yard. *C'est formidable!* Talk about grand entrances. I liked to look at the Widener steps but climbing them was something else. And once inside you had yet another grand staircase to enjoy. I did roam the translucent floors of the stacks from time to time, but my best reading was about a hundred feet away, in a more utilitarian structure that sat comfortably on a corner of the Yard. We called it after its donor's name: Lamont.

No Quonset hut, this. (Harvard has always known what size and shape it would be, regardless of wars and veterans.) Rather a modern red stone building of three or four stories, one of them below ground level, presumably to keep its profile no higher than the President's House just across the walk from it. It was not only a reading room for reserved items but a reference library of major standard works by disciplines, often in multiple copies. But what a wonderful place to get away to.

This time it wasn't only Saturday afternoons, it was any time that could be stolen from seminars and dissertation work. And it wasn't a more or less irrelevant interest in a certain kind of sociology but a somewhat relevant interest in a certain kind of political theory, namely ancient and medieval, fields that I did *not* offer for the oral exams.

While doing course work in theory, for example, I encountered the almost archaeological bent of Werner Jaeger (as translated by Gilbert Highet) in *Paideia*, his three-volume masterpiece on the shaping of the Greek character. Jaeger focused on heroic, civic, and political personalities and on the struggle, during Plato's time, between the intellect on one side and culture and the state on the other. A central concept for him was *arete*, a combination of proud and courtly morality with heroic valour, a notion of human and even non-human excellence. After reading Jaeger on *arete* it felt good just to say the word.

It seemed that the more exotic the subject matter—or perhaps the further from the academic everyday—the more I enjoyed it. I've also thought of it as a sort of intellectual wanderlust, a strong longing to travel in the geographies of an author's mind that were far from my own. But then it could have been nothing more than a small piece of graduate-school perversity: if they're going to make me read these dreadful syntheses in the histories of political thought, I'm going to get my own back by indulging freely when they mention something in passing that really appeals to me.

Take Marsiglio of Padua and Nicholas of Cusa on authority, for instance, or William of Occam on property and lordship. Ewart Lewis had translated them and many others in her two-volume *Medieval Political Ideas*, preceding each section of translations with her own brilliant essays. As between the histories of ideas and the original writings of the thinkers, I went for the latter. It was good clean fun to read Occam "beg and entreat" his reader to "deign to show me my error" and then try to figure out from what follows whether he was pulling the reader's leg or doing the required false-modesty jig of the time.

Several years later my time with *Medieval Political Ideas* took a nice turn. I was invited to interview for a position in the Government Department at Oberlin College. The chairman was kind enough to meet me at the airport and drive me back to the college for interviews. He suggested we stop at his home for a relaxed hour before going on to the college. As we entered the house the chairman, John Lewis by name, turned to me and said, "I want you to meet my wife, Ewart." It was part of the vagaries of the academic world at that time that Ewart Lewis was the editor of a major anthology in political theory but held no academic appointment.

Reading with a Vengeance

After a while, then, when I was obliged to write a dissertation, the delights of the reading room gave way to the dim lights of the research cubicle. I never became habituated to the innards of Widener, however, because my subject, in comparative government and politics, allowed for travel. That could be put the other way around, I suppose: my interest in travel, especially in Europe, accommodated a dissertation in comparative government and politics.

Either way, the outcome was the same: a year abroad, at Heidelberg University. My general subject was federalism and my particular interest was in the way the German politicians and constitutional lawyers resolved conflicts between the provincial and national authorities in both the Weimar and Bonn republics. As a specific case I chose the relationship between the two levels of government in deciding which was to have responsibility for the development and, most importantly, control of radio broadcasting. It wasn't exactly a burning issue, but it was contentious in both periods. I did detailed research. No one had covered that ground before. (Nor, I suspect, will anyone again.)

And it was not unpleasant. I honed my German and spent many hours in the university archives. Once again I avoided the *Big Library*, this time because a large part of my work on the Weimar period was done in the newspapers of the time, particularly the *Frankfurter Allgemeine* and the *Suddeutsche Zeitung*, and they were housed separately from the main collection.

It was library work, but of a rather intense sort, quite unlike my recreational approach to Howard Becker's essays or Ewart Lewis's documents and analyses. My overall time was limited and the sheer volume of scanning, reading, and note-taking was daunting. Fortunately, there were no copying machines; if there had been I'm sure I would have gotten only half as much reading done. I adapted to the typefaces of the German press in the 20s and 30s and learned quickly to locate where, within a page or two in any given issue, I would find the relevant news items, feature articles, and commentaries.

A dissertation probably brings out something unexpected in everyone who does one. Some people learn to write (though, obviously, not all). I learned to read very intensively. I have never read that intensively since.

A small, slightly related anecdote, if I may? While in Heidelberg I got in touch with a distant cousin, a graduate student in philology at Freiburg University. We agreed that I would go to her building at the university on a certain day and the concierge would relay a message to her. She soon appeared and laughingly told me how my arrival had been received.

There was, she said, a standing joke among graduate students who, when they wanted to leave a meeting early, would say, "Entschuldigen Sie, bitte; mein Vetter aus Amerika ist angekommen." ("Please excuse me; my cousin from America has arrived.") She happened to be in a seminar session when told I was waiting and, to hoots and catcalls, she rose dramatically and said, of course, "Entschuldigen Sie, bitte; mein Vetter aus Amerika ist angekommen."

A Writing Room

As a writer today, I am the Siamese twin to my PC, joined at the keyboard. Where it plugs in, I plug in the content. Prior to twinning with the PC, however, I found many places to write by hand or typewriter. The kitchen table, the dining-room table, a tutor's room furnished with a desk and two chairs, a bedroom with a card table, an honest-to-goodness book-lined study, a professorial office, an administrative office. But I had not written in a library until I joined the Oberlin faculty and later was invited to do a case study of the town's fair-housing ordinance for a book of such studies. Oberlin's ordinance was the first in the country to be found constitutional.

The town of Oberlin, located a few miles south of Lake Erie and southwest of Cleveland, Ohio, had been a special place in the history of race relations in the north. Prior to the Civil War it was an important way station on the Underground Railroad for escaped slaves moving up from the south and around the lake into Canada. As happened in other towns that served the Underground Railroad, from time to time a few of the escapees would settle instead of continuing on their route.

In this way black communities emerged within these rather small, predominantly white towns. In Oberlin's case the numbers were large enough that in the years right after the Civil War it had, in percentage terms, the largest black population in any community in Ohio. That population was concentrated in the southeast quarter, a pattern that persisted through the decades and set the stage for the battle against segregation that emerged in the '50s and '60s. I began by interviewing town and college leaders, but soon began spending most of my time in the college library, which has a rich collection on racial issues in the town's and the college's history.

It took several weeks of lugging documents back and forth between library, office, and home before I decided to try writing at the library. I didn't think it would work. Despite all the reading and writing I had done, the two activities seemed oddly incompatible. What I liked about *home* and *office* was the solitude and the personal mobility. No one interrupted, and I could pace or make a cup of coffee when a sentence seemed especially ungainly. What I liked about *library* was density and availability. I could find what I wanted and then use it or take it away.

It didn't go well at first. I arranged for a study, actually an enclosed cubicle with a small writing surface and two shelves above it, and brought in a typewriter. My first few paragraphs felt like failed writing exercises and the next few weren't very good either. After a few days, as the shelves filled up with materials checked out to the study, I began to feel comfortable. Once I closed the door the solitude was there, even more so than anywhere else; there was no telephone and no knock on the door. The paragraphs became acceptable and even publishable.

It was the separateness in the midst of plenty that did it. If I needed a reference it was at hand. Family and friends, colleagues and students were safely elsewhere. Only one thing happened in that study, the drafting of an article on the fair-housing ordinance. I looked forward to the trip across campus to reach my cubicle and enjoyed closing the door behind me. I was focused!

Oberlin's library of that time, incidentally, was, like Joseph Mann, a member of the large family of Carnegies. It was built in 1908 with a grant of about $150,000 from the donor and named after him. Oberlin's Carnegie, too, has been recycled, though not so abruptly that a FOR LEASE sign decorates it. It still has two floors of stacks, and there is a science department on the top floor, but the traditional high-ceilinged reading room now can be rented for social functions.

Back to the Future

I stopped teaching a few years ago in order to spend more time on music, but I find my way back to *library* in rather different ways. There was that gig I did a few years ago with the Canal Street Jazz Band at the New York Public Library on Fifth Avenue. American Express engaged us to entertain at a reception on the main floor for the opening exhibit of what would be a national tour of baseball memorabilia. The event was a success but the acoustics were terrible! I've also visited the New York Public Library branch at Lincoln Center from time to time to use the sheet music collection or the fake-book collection, looking for the original chord changes on an Ellington piece or an obscure 1920s pop tune.

More often I've walked from my building down Flatbush Avenue for five blocks to a tiny neighborhood branch of the Brooklyn Public Library, there to scan the *Wall Street Journal* or *Barron's* financial weekly for practical advice on how to retain the *enormous* wealth accumulated during an academic career. The branch's hours are different every day, presumably to accommodate the budgetary needs of the city government rather than the needs of readers. I find that if I arrive before two o'clock on Monday, Tuesday, or Thursday I don't have to wear ear plugs against the din from the preteens who take over at that hour. The din itself isn't so bad—it's a pretty happy sound in a library—but I don't like to stand while reading.

My most recent visits have been to that new library on the lake in Two Rivers. One must, after all, read the *New York Times* every day, and you can't get it at a newstand in that town. And while there, sitting in the periodicals lounge, just across from the fireplace, why not catch up on the *Milwaukee Journal* for the past week, not to mention the *Two Rivers Reporter*.

Once a Librarian...

Janet Freedman

Janet Freedman, Dean of Libraries, University of Massachusetts–Dartmouth, is currently serving on the board of the New Bedford Women's Center, Bedford, Massachusetts, and co-directing a university-community partnership for the Center for Jewish Culture for southeastern Massachusetts.

I no longer go to work each day as a librarian. Three years ago I opted to focus on my other love, classroom teaching, and gave up the position I held as Dean of Library Services at the University of Massachusetts–Dartmouth to teach full-time and direct the university's women's studies program. But "once a librarian," I continue to be inspired by the vision and practice of social change I learned through my work in libraries.

An invitation to contribute to a collection of essays on the profession can prompt nostalgia—a romanticizing of the past. Probably because my mother had been a librarian, I played "library" the way some children play school, but I certainly didn't aspire to the work she did until, as she put it, "your father rescued me from the stacks."

No, my career choice was one of default, consistent with the observation that Helen Lowenthal made in an excellent article written when librarianship began to feel the effects of a growing feminist movement. Like Helen and many others who sought a career prior to the "second wave" of the women's movement, my profession chose me. I attended college in the early '60s just before the movement opened a fuller range of choices for women. Simmons College, where I earned my bachelor's and master's degrees, was created with the pioneering notion that women should have meaningful careers, but founded at a time when the opportunities for women workers were concentrated in the "semi-professions": nursing, social work, teaching, librarianship. Since I had to choose from among these, librarianship seemed the best of the lot. Simmons changed a few years after I graduated. It still prepares women for the work world and the quality programs have challenged Amitai Etzioni's notion of what constitutes "professional." But now its undergraduates routinely enter medical and law school, too.

I changed, too. As the '60s progressed, the social and political climate influenced how I approached my work. But looking back, my experiences at a women's college, and the issues raised by some of my library school colleagues and faculty made me open to participation in the movements of that and the next decade.

I recall one example that raised my awareness of the power of information. The library school presented a display of what might have been categorized then as extremist literature (although, to my horror, many of the viewpoints have become mainstream). The exhibit led to my request to do an independent research project on the John Birch Society, a progenitor of today's flourishing right wing. One of the men I interviewed at the organization's headquarters in Belmont, Massachusetts, boasted about the effectiveness of the "One Dozen Candles," twelve books that were sent as gifts to libraries. In many of the small collections that accepted the volumes, these became the only perspective on particular topics. I learned that the profession I was entering was a powerful one, that what was included—or left out—of a library collection could have enormous influence, and I pledged to include a wide range of opinions and expressions in the libraries where I would work.

This became a major focus of my work as public services librarian at Salem State College where I spent about a decade of my professional life. One of my favorite projects was the Alternatives Library, a library-within-the-library, created with the help of a work-study student who later went on to library school and became a fabulous librarian. The facility offered a broad range of books, journals, pamphlets and "ephemera" that were not readily available in the college or other libraries. Students requested and I sought out information on topics of interest and concern to them; students also determined how they wished the collection to be organized and staffed, publicized the facility and generated programming, from poetry readings to political discussions.

In those days, I was likely to be found in overalls, sitting on the floor with a student strategizing how to locate relevant resources within the A/L or in the "regular" collection, in other libraries, community agencies and from knowledgeable individuals. When we discovered a helpful community or human resource, we added it to a growing file that could be used, and added to, by other students. We were able to acquire and sustain funding from the student government and the comfortable furnishings and warm environment of the A/L attracted more students to this facility than to the traditional reference desk. The collection became a starting point for many students to choose a topic for a paper and I soon began to meet individual students and classes in this space and then introduce them to the catalogs, indexes and other reference tools and sources.

I recalled—and shared with those I helped—how clueless I had been about information searching prior to my first courses in library school. I wanted to share all that I could and demystify the process of finding and using information. (I still can't resist pursuing someone who, after checking the public catalog, shrugs and starts to walk out of the library.)

A colleague and I soon collaborated to develop a course on information searching and media communication. Harold Bantly was as tall as I was short— and as apolitical as I was politically involved. He was, is, a person of great intelligence, talent, integrity and he taught me, and together we taught our students, the value of all forms of media to capture information and present it to others. Although the course was intended to help students with their formal academic program, we encouraged them to begin with their own interests in investigating the world of information. We started, not with what they *should* know, but with what they *did* know, and we discovered that nearly every person in the classes qualified as an expert in one area or another and could aid her/his classmates with their research. Students also learned to use 35 mm cameras, and audio and video recorders when these were appropriate to gather data, and to edit these records in preparing and delivering presentations.

With the help of a Council on Library Resources/National Endowment for the Humanities grant, the course became part of a unified freshman year program with the required History of Western Civilization, Speech and English courses. Eventually, we were asked to develop some sections for students deemed in need of "remedial" skills. Every class developed a community of learners who discovered information tools and resources, exchanged helpful and not-so-successful search strategies and explored the social and political environment in which information was generated and disseminated. Discovering the root of the word "propaganda," in Pope Gregory XV's 1622 *Congregation for Propagating the Faith*, students considered how the intentional diffusion of particular ideas influenced all cultures throughout history, including our own democratic society. We considered what got published and what didn't and why. We showed the film *I. F. Stone's Weekly* and students were inspired by that information sleuth whose careful reading of newspapers and congressional reports caught the government in its own lies.

This was an era when cable television was offering great promise as the medium for "the people." As required by federal legislation, cities and towns were sponsoring workshops for residents who would then be able to broadcast their group's projects, spreading information and expanding community. We envisioned a more responsive and responsible government connected to the living rooms of folks whose increased awareness would lead to more active participation in shaping their own lives and communities. The compromised expectations of this "wired nation" make me skeptical about the promises of this generation's technology. What is heralded to bring about a global village, with its connotation of intimate community, can create, instead, the spread of ideological and economic control by those with power and influence. But more about this later…

At the end of the '60s and in the early '70s, some of us spoke about "revolutionary" librarianship. Support and encouragement for that concept was available from ALA's Social Responsibility Round Table (SRRT), which sponsored working groups on feminism, gay and lesbian issues, workers rights and other concerns, and gathered *Alternatives-in-Print* to apprise librarians of hard-to-identify literature that should be considered for their collections. *Synergy*, the lively publication birthed at the San Francisco Public Library, and its superb successor, *Booklegger*, provided further inspiration. I submitted an article to the latter and formed a lasting friendship with its editor, Celeste West, who introduced me to sisters from Canada who were creating a network of progressive librarians there through a journal called *Emergency Librarian*. Feminist energy coalesced through ALA's Committee on the Status of Women in Libraries, SRRT's Feminist Task Force and the Association of College and Research Libraries women's section. A new organization, Women Library Workers, was created to reach all information workers, not just "professionals," and produced an information-packed journal. A conference on *Women in a Women's Profession*, brought many of these activists together and produced a directory of feminist librarians willing to provide mutual aid. S.H.A.R.E. (Sisters Have Resources Everywhere) was compiled by the same woman who is editing this collection of essays!

My most important professional network at that time was the Boston Area Women in Libraries. Our enthusiasm for the organization made us less thoughtful about the acronym than we might have been, but BAWIL *was* quite a movement! Donna Polhamus (librarian in the Lexington, Massachusetts, school system) was a principal in creating a wonderful slide/tape program on images of girls and women in children's literature that was first shown at the Massachusetts Library Association's annual conference, and then presented at many schools and libraries. Another project developed a series of bibliographies on topics of interest to women and their friends. Separate resource guides on divorce, abortion, child care, lesbianism and other topics were enclosed in a folder that opened to become a poster created by one of our talented members. The poster proclaimed *This Library Is a Feminist Resource Center* and we hoped our colleagues would purchase the materials that could make that the case. Our gatherings led to the development of close friendships, offering very real support through personal and professional challenges. One of the members of the group shared my home after my divorce;

she was asked by and became my five-year-old daughter's "best friend," and introduced me to my beloved, Andrew.

Another energizing connection came from my involvement in the American Friends Service Committee. I had worked with the AFSC in anti–Vietnam War activities and was pleased when its Vocations for Social Change project sponsored a Librarian's Work Group. Our regular meetings gave us a chance to explore ways to connect our daily work to social change. In this setting we learned that almost everything we did in our worklives could make a difference, from seeing to it that materials by and about all members of our society are in our libraries and that they are described in ways that do not diminish the humanity of any group. Some of the most important work of that period was done by catalogers who changed subject headings, such as those that described women as exceptions and gays and lesbians as sexual deviants. Librarians were involved in creating new access tools—"people's yellow pages"—and community resource files such as that developed for the Alternatives Library. Displays, lectures, film series, instructional programs, interactions with users at the reference desk—all had the potential for social and political change. And so did the ways in which we interacted with colleagues and reached out to make alliances with other community workers.

But a funny thing happened on the way to the revolution. As my years at Salem State College passed, the programs that I created as "alternatives" became celebrated by the very traditional agencies that I thought I was challenging. The integrated curriculum was awarded recognition by the American Association of State Colleges and Universities as one of the top ten curriculum innovations of the year; the Alternatives Library was toured by trustees of the public college system. I learned firsthand what I had understood intellectually. In American culture "radicalism" (for that is what I thought I was about) is easily co-opted and often repackaged and marketed in a way that maintains the position and values of the dominant culture.

It was time to move on. Andy and I decided to move with my two daughters to a community where we could affirm our new family unit. That brought me to the University of Massachusetts–Dartmouth, then Southeastern Massachusetts University, where I became director of the university library, a position that was then retitled Dean of Library Services. I was nervous. Although I had coordinated projects and directed small units, this position made me a member of the academic leadership team, the Council of Academic Deans. I was the first woman among the public college and university library directors. I had shed my overalls for a business suit but was dismayed when one of my "fellow" academic library directors called to say he was happy I'd given up my radical ideas. I had not and, although I made many mistakes in the eighteen years of leading the library at UMass-Dartmouth, I did not waver from my vision of the library as a center for empowerment and social change.

"Directing," from my perspective, was assuring that staff members had support and resources to do excellent work. I spoke forcefully, and successfully, in defending the library's budget in difficult fiscal times, advocated for the people in my unit, gaining approval for all promotion and tenure recommendations for professional staff and upgrades for classified personnel, and linked the library to the community in many ways, including free borrowing privileges. I am proud of the fact that I worked openly and consciously as a feminist and spoke with a woman's voice in all my interactions with students, staff, administration and community. I was and am inspired by Ursula LeGuin's comments on the "mother tongue," in which language is used "not as mere communication, but as relation, relationship. It connects."

Making authentic connections has been essential to my work, whether it is an "assignment" to represent the university administration at a community event, or my own choices of involvement, such as service on the board of the New Bedford Women's Center and co-directing a university-community partnership, the Center for Jewish Culture, that seeks to enrich the educational and cultural opportunities of the small Jewish communities in southeastern Massachusetts.

In the '60s and '70s it seemed that a mass movement for social change was possible, and I joined in large demonstrations against the war in Vietnam and for civil rights and women's liberation. But even in those heady times, I believed that change depended more on integrating political ideology into everyday practices than in demonstrations. Today there is a dearth of mass organizing for progressive political and social action, so it is vital to invest in the "small" changes that can lead to other, more widespread and deeper changes. This perspective is articulated well by Bettina Aptheker in her book, *Tapestries of Life*. She reveals how the literature, art, family and worklives of women are shaped by everyday events and relationships, as opposed to the dramatic adventures or heroic individual acts that characterize traditional notions of change. Aptheker urges us to become self conscious about the ways in which we can and do make a difference through our "ordinary" actions.

The ordinary is not the opposite of the extraordinary, but the most important component of that word. Librarianship offers abundant opportunities for transforming individual lives, communities and societies through what we do each day. Throughout my career, I have joined those who realize and claim this power. But I have often been disappointed by the efforts of my colleagues to gain recognition, not by claiming their own unique professional skills, but with and through other groups that they perceive to be more influential. One example of this is the enormous time and energy academic librarians have expended on achieving faculty status. Of course, librarians are indispensable teachers and I take for granted that we should be considered faculty, but these efforts often are rooted in wanting "to be like" another group, rather than in a sense of self-worth that grows from a vision of the role we librarians have in maintaining and enlarging freedom.

As a group, librarians can be an important voice in confronting misinformation, disinformation and the horrific social inequities of the technological "revolution." Yet many prefer to identify as "information scientists," and tech talk has subsumed conversation about social responsibility. With little debate as to the real value of the systems and hardware that consume the majority of most library budgets, some librarians have become sycophants applauding the "information age," ignoring the fact that presumed abundance masks the fact that we are receiving more information about consumer goods than meaningful, in-depth knowledge. What better group than librarians to model a deeper, more thoughtful analysis of both the ways in which technology can enhance—or control—what we know and to insist that the potential of the Internet, like the earlier cable technologies, be an instrument for education, participation, and empowerment.

I am still passionate about the power of information—useful information that can awaken human possibilities for living, working and learning. Although the "global economy" has centralized the control of information in ways that seemed inconceivable a few years ago, I try to resist and help others resist the commodity-driven vision of "information" that is now being spread through the Internet. In the classroom, just as at the reference desk in earlier years of my career, I have the joy of observing how a desire to learn and grow can overcome the acceptance of the easy or simple answer.

My enthusiasm for cable television in the early '70s was based on a sincere belief that technology "for the people" was possible. It wasn't long, however, before I realized how much energy and organizing would be needed to provide awareness and skills that would give the average citizen a voice. An important part of the team-taught course described above covered the legislation that permitted public access to cable and encouraged students to use their local station to create their own programming. At the same time, students had an opportunity to study how information was structured in this and other societies. They were appalled to learn the extent of censorship and disinformation in totalitarian regimes, and also were shocked to realize that the free flow of information in our democratic state could be challenged by a shift in the political proclivities of those who control the interlocking ownership of publishing, cable television, and other mechanisms for communication. An awareness of the context in which information is created and distributed, combined with real skills in accessing, evaluating and presenting information, made them knowledgeable users and creators of information and, perhaps, more committed to work for a notion of democracy that values people as much as profits.

Teaching how to find, evaluate, use, and share information remains an important part of my everyday work for personal and social change. As director of the women's studies program, I am planning with faculty ways to integrate these skills into the women's studies curriculum. The introduction to the women's studies course will be built around the critical use of information, and all women's studies students will have an opportunity to participate in workshops in the computer lab we have created in the Women's Resource Center. The theoretical perspectives of the academic program are linked to a myriad of campus and community projects, all of which rest upon thoughtful, research-based analysis using library, Internet, human and community sources that can inform strategies and actions.

A few weeks ago, the Dean of Instruction at a college in another part of the state brought his daughter for an interview at UMass-Dartmouth. The dean was the student who so many years ago was my "comrade in struggle" in the creation of the Alternatives Library. He dropped by the Women's Resource Center where I was working with colleagues on a grant proposal. As he walked through our suite, he laughed appreciatively at the prints and posters on the walls, some of which had decorated the Alternatives Library. "You haven't changed a bit, Janet," he said. And, though I know I have and hope to continue to grow and change in my personal journey to be/come all that I can be, it is true that my vision of social change has remained the same. That is why one of the familiar mementos he noted was the excerpt from a poem by Marge Piercy, that I still keep above my desk. Its final line reads: "The pitcher cries for water to carry / And a person for work that is real" (*Circles on the Water: Selected Poems of Marge Piercy*. New York: Knopf, 1982, p. 106).

Librarianship is real work, useful, "everyday" work that can advance social change in so many and important ways. So, although the classroom is the new setting for what I do each day, I'll always be a librarian!

Works Cited

Aptheker, Bettina. *Tapestries of Life.* Amherst: University of Massachusetts Press, 1989.

Etzioni, Amitai. *Semi-Professions: Nursing, Social Work, Teaching, Librarianship.* New York: Free Press, 1969.

LeGuin, Ursula. (Commencement Address). Bryn Mawr College, Bryn Mawr, PA, 1986.

Lowenthal, Helen. "A Healthy Anger." *Library Journal* 1 Sept. 1971: 2597–99.

Piercy, Marge. *Circles on the Water: Selected Poems.* New York: Knopf, 1982.

Social Equity and Empowerment in the Digital Age: A Place for Activist Librarians

Carla J. Stoffle

Carla J. Stoffle has been a committed social activist and librarian since she was a Peace Corps volunteer in the 1960s. She is currently Dean of the University of Arizona Libraries and the Center for Creative Photography.

A great deal has been written about the library as a safety net in the digital environment. It is often described as the safety net which exists primarily to maintain physical access to equipment, connections, software, and information in print and electronic form for the economically disadvantaged in American society. Librarians appear to have reached ready agreement on this concept because it grows out of the library's traditional activities. However, there is a place and a need for social activists and social activism in libraries that goes beyond the foregoing concepts and resulting activities. Today's new environment gives librarians a second chance at providing access and legitimization to those communities that our libraries have served less well in the past few decades. This essay describes what some of these roles for library social activists are and how they have been exercised in one academic environment. It goes on to propose how others in different types of library organizations can create an environment where the library and individual librarians can effectively act on their social responsibilities in their communities.

Though the emphasis on this essay is on our new digital environment, this does not mean that I forsake print or the library as a physical space. Libraries are essential as a gathering places for virtual and literal conversations.

Librarians teach new millennium skills like digital information literacy and provide access to physical texts like the papers of Father Kino, a man who played a crucial role in the lives of all peoples of the Southwest. Print and technology will always enhance one another. I applaud increases in our state budget for books. At the University of Arizona Library, we have placed many of our fund-raising efforts on book collections. We are particularly interested in collecting materials that demonstrate our richly textured southwest region, with its many landscapes and ethnic groups.

Personal History of Activism

Before I begin, I should confess that I have been committed always to an activist role for librarians. My commitment to activism probably started with my Peace Corps experience where I first came to understand the importance of the library to people who did not have ready access to information. This commitment has been apparent throughout my career by the development of socially responsible library programs in the various libraries where I have worked, by my exercise of social responsibility in the decisions I have made and the priorities I have set, and in my writing about library services. While my career has been in academic libraries, and I write from this experience, my commitment to expanding library social roles was evidenced in my first article written in library school about public library services to the disadvantaged (Stoffle, 1969). This article was intended to guide those seeking new ideas and to stimulate and reinforce the social role of libraries and librarians. It was my intent to validate and document social responsibility in libraries.

In my first academic library experience at Eastern Kentucky University, I developed library instruction programs focused on helping students find and use government information. I viewed my responsibility as one that included reaching out to faculty and students and bringing them to the library to solve information problems. While at the University of Wisconsin–Parkside, I supported the development of the Reference Assistance Project (Piele and Yamel, 1982) using students of color as reference assistants and as role models; the creation of a program which involved the library in a summer program designed to prepare students of color in junior high and high school for college admission; the implementation of a socially sensitive and outreach-focused library instruction program; the establishment of an active affirmative action program within and without the library, and the library's involvement in campus and community outreach services designed to improve access and make the library a more vital part of its local community. At the University of Michigan Library, a Peer Information Counseling Program (PIC) was among the numerous programs initiated to provide socially responsible, activist library services;

statements on diversity and the value of diversity in the services, programs, staff, and collections were developed and followed (Stoffle and Tarin). These programs have become models for other institutions and won for the library the first University of Michigan Diversity Award.

While I am proud of these examples of socially responsive librarianship, the following essay focuses on my University of Arizona Library experiences and my belief in the potential of the electronic environment for extending the impact of social responsibility.

New Roles

Neither the library as a safety net nor the library as a gateway in the new digital environment is a concept that has great appeal to me. I do not think that they will lead to the creation of viable, sustaining activities that will best serve our public over time. In assuming that libraries are simply applying new technologies to old tasks and dreading the mythical dehumanization that is often predicted as a result, librarians are selling ourselves and our communities short.

We must view the new environment as one filled with opportunity for our communities and us. Essentially, the new telecommunications and information technologies are transforming the whole knowledge creation process. They are affecting the fundamental structure and work of our society, and especially the work of librarians. To see these new technologies as less than that is to lose the greatest opportunity for serving society since the invention of the printing press. Such short sightedness will allow others who do not share our values and philosophical commitment to information as a public good to usurp and replace us.

Then what roles should we play? As Jesse Shera put it in 1969, "The purpose of the Library is to maximize the social utility of the graphic record" (Shera, 1965). Using this as a guide, our roles are then centered on the creation, management, and transmission of information, knowledge and culture. Thus, I would propose that librarians must move from reference, acquisitions, cataloging, and management of physical facilities to education and knowledge management/electronic publishing. A knowledge manager is someone who not only organizes information, but who engages in the creation of new knowledge packages (publishing) and new access tools (Stoffle, 1996). By educator, I mean someone who undertakes creating an environment where learning takes place as the highest priority (Stoffle, 1995). Making the public self-sufficient, not dependent on knowledge intermediaries, is a primary goal; so is outreach and activism in service to our customers. These values characterize our behaviors.

New Technology's Role in Reaching Those Who Have Been Traditionally Underserved by Libraries

Generally, in the past, our libraries have been more a reflection and reinforcer of the dominant culture. We have focused on socializing or educating non-traditional populations to adopt the values and beliefs of the dominant culture. With a few exceptions, we have not provided legitimization or understanding of alternative cultures or lifestyles. For example, as Sandy Berman has been telling us for years, we blindly use Library of Congress subject headings which are biased toward the dominant culture (Berman, 1993) and do not acknowledge the negative social impact of our actions on others in the community. In the new digital environment we have thus far continued to use these with the same consequences. However, we could get around these limiting factors by encouraging the use of keyword searching, which is more expansive and inclusive, through simply placing it first in our menu of search choices or more actively teaching keyword searching to our public. This would be a more socially responsible action. Also, we generally have purchased print materials published by the mainstream presses, indexed by the major indexes, and reviewed by the major journals. We have been limited in our collection to materials that were commercially viable and we have continued these practices into the digital environment. Unfortunately, these, in general, do not reflect the history or culture of a growing segment of our population, at least from their point of view. For the most part, our non-mainstream citizens/students do not see themselves in our major public and academic libraries and their collections.

The new education and knowledge management roles give us a chance to start over. We can reinvent ourselves using the knowledge, values, skills, and relationships we have developed over time. We do not have to be limited by either our historical physical collections or the constraints of an access system (LC headings) that has outlived its usefulness. As knowledge managers (publishers), we can ensure that the new environment provides access to the literature and histories of all segments of our society. As we band together to identify and make available materials in digitized form we can and must include literature that is not necessarily commercially viable but which allows other segments of our society to see themselves and to be legitimized.

An example of what I am talking about is the "Through Our Parents' Eyes" (http://dizzy.library.arizona.edu:80/images/diverse/diverse.html) project at the University of Arizona Library. "Through Our Parents' Eyes" is an important community outreach program. The digital projects are overseen by editors from the University of Arizona in collaboration with librarians for the community college and the state's historical museums. The heart of the exhibits is oral history. The quality of the materials on the Web sites is outstanding. This is a project designed to make available over the Internet materials dealing with the history and culture of the various ethnic groups that make up the Tucson community. It has thus far involved digitizing materials from the university library's and Arizona State Historical Society's collections, materials from local community groups, and even materials from a summer teen project that created oral histories from interviews with community members. All of these materials are finding use in the local schools as well as in university courses that focus on the Southwest. We attempt to highlight "Through Our Parents' Eyes" when we are teaching library skills and have made this project a focus of many of our public relations and outreach programs. Also, families who are interested in communicating the history of their culture to their children have let us know that our online exhibits have been invaluable. It is particularly important to put socially responsible material like "Through Our Parents' Eyes" on the World Wide Web. It increases the visibility of the work and experiences of those outside our dominant culture.

In addition to creating materials described above, by adopting the publisher role, librarians can help break the inelastic market now controlled by a small band of commercial publishers. This market has acted to increase prices and limit access to information. The result is that small publishers are often forced out of business. It is the same market that is trying to control the Internet with restrictive copyright policies, licensing restrictions which inappropriately attempt to control who can use our libraries, and encryption devices to identify and potentially bill users for even viewing information. By breaking this market monopoly, we can ensure broad access to information. The University of Arizona Library has taken a few steps in this direction by working with the Society for Molecular Biology and Evolution, the Society for Range Management, and the Percussive Arts Society to digitize the back files of the journals so that they are free or available at low cost to libraries. We have also joined with other libraries to form buying consortia that have adopted socially responsible licensing guidelines. We have developed collection policies that punish, by deselecting titles of those publishers who constantly raise prices at unjustifiable levels. Also, with regard to document delivery, the library has adopted a no charge policy and has established practices that cap the amount the library is willing to pay in copyright fees. Finally, the library has become a founding member of SPARC, the Scholarly Publishing and Academic Resource Coalition (ARL, 1998), which creates partnerships with nonprofit and commercial publishers to reduce journal costs.

As knowledge managers, librarians can recast forms of access to better serve our diverse communities. This is a task that we have left to vendors and technicians who have less knowledge of the end user. Equity of access is not simply a matter of treating everyone the same. It is ensuring that our policies and access tools take into account individual and group differences.

How information will be consistently retrieved from the networks is a problem that has not been solved. By participating in its solution we can help our users and overcome the inadequacies of our present retrieval systems. We really have a responsibility to actively undertake this task. Libraries, including the University of Arizona Library, are adopting search tools such as Sitesearch. This allows the library to overlay existing systems with new terminology and generalized access systems allowing one to use a variety of databases without having to learn many new systems. We are also accepting responsibility for helping the campus manage its information through such systems. All of this provides increased access for the public and removes the barriers of classification systems and archaic subject structures.

The educational role of the library and the librarian has been debated for the last 100 years. The concept of the role has evolved from teaching how to use the library, to teaching how to use bibliographic tools, to teaching how to think about information systems, strategies, and policies. However, even with its current acceptance, the educational role of the library has never consumed more than a small portion of the library's resources. More time has gone into creating systems which required librarians as intermediaries. The new information environment, with the emergence of virtual universities and just-in-time learning programs, not only provides the opportunity, but demands that we abolish mediation in many of our services. We must devote the precious knowledge and skill of the librarian not only to teach about information but also to work in conjunction with other educators to design active, learning experiences in a variety of settings for our diverse students. At the University of Arizona, the library is engaging in a massive project to establish librarians as partners in the educational process from course design through class evaluation. Librarians are in some cases co-teachers and in others provide help in designing projects that make students active learners. Nearly 100 workshops to enhance student identified skills are made available each semester. An online tutorial called RIO (Research Instruction Online) (http://dizzy.library.arizona.edu/rio/) is now available and over 1000 sessions for individual classes are being taught. An evaluation program is being developed. An automated online reserve system enhances the learning process. This system creates Web pages for each course with passworded online readings. The faculty member can add to the system at any time and can tell whether students are reading the material or not.

In addition to designing new learning programs, librarians must ensure that such programs use examples that broadly represent the literature and the experience of all our citizens. As we reach into each classroom and teach about the information structure, we must be sure to help our communities find, appreciate, and use the writings of authors from under-represented populations and their literature. We must help the dominant as well as the under-represented culture see a broader society. These principles are basic to the instructional programs at the University of Arizona Library.

We must still extend our educational role even further. We must take on educating our communities about the broader implications of the new technologies and the national information policies being developed. We must ensure that our communities understand the dangers in limiting access and we must help them see the implications of an information-based economy that leaves out a growing proportion of our society. We must protect privacy and limit fees as we face new situations with demands that we have never had to deal with before. Many academic libraries are meeting these challenges by encouraging faculty and faculty committees to talk about these issues. At the University of Arizona Library, I chair a Faculty Senate Committee on Intellectual Property and Scholarly Communication. I also sit on the Information Technology Council. In addition, the library has undertaken a campaign to visit each college and department over the next year to raise the awareness of the faculty and create an environment that is ready to exercise socially responsible information policies.

Finally, as we pursue our educational role, we cannot simply wait for people to come to the library to be taught. Simply offering and advertising these services is not enough. We must reach out and go to the neighborhoods, clubs, and dorms where our non-traditional community members reside. We must design special instructions based on how different communities learn. We must design activities that invite and encourage people of color to come to our libraries and we must be sure that our environment says that they are welcome and wanted. The University of Arizona Library created a Peer Information Counseling Program mentioned earlier that trains students of color in the use of information resources. To make the library more inviting and secure for students of color, members of the PIC work at the reference desk and in the residence halls. These students also participate and help develop outreach programs for the library. We work with campus organizations as co-sponsors of film festivals, speakers, and other such programs and we provide space and support for groups when particularly sensitive subjects or problems are being addressed.

How Must We Change?

We must redefine our organizations and change the way that we work. If we flattened our organizations we could free up resources and increase flexibility to meet the needs of our diverse customers. We cannot justify lack of change or activism based on needing to use current resources to maintain traditional activities.

We must hire and develop a diverse workforce at all levels of the organization. Frankly, if we cannot create a good working environment for a diverse staff, we have no hope of creating a library/information environment that is inviting to our underserved populations. We must rethink the work of the library and how we use the budget to accomplish our work. We will not get new dollars for most of the changes we have to make. Thus, we must make hard choices about priorities, streamline and reduce the complexity of our work, and look at value added from the customer point of view. We must adopt a continuous learning mode and a commitment to continually improving our services. We must reduce the cycle time of introducing new services and create an environment that encourages risk-taking. We must create partnerships with other educators, information professionals, vendors, and commercial interests to create the systems necessary to serve a diverse public.

The University of Arizona Library has done the above and more. The library is organized to reflect how our customers work. We have made customer service our number one goal and have structured our activities to identify customer needs and to design programs that meet those needs. We elicit customer feedback and have a library report card in which customer grades determine a dollar bonus for library staff. We have used quality management techniques to reduce the cost of services while improving their quality. Within the last four years, the library has reduced reshelving time from 60 hours to less than 10 hours; reduced the time it takes to get books ordered from 40-plus days to 24 hours; reduced the time it takes to get new books to the stacks from four weeks to four days; and reduced interlibrary loan delivery time from five weeks to less than one week. While doing this, the library has been able to reallocate over $300,000 to: improving staff and student worker salaries; hiring additional librarians, including copyright, knowledge management and meta data librarians.

Within these changes, the library has made diversity a high priority in hiring. For professional development and training, staff are given the equivalent of one month per year individually as released time. No one has been laid off or lost a job due to these changes. All of these activities are good for business, but they also promote social responsibility because they create inclusive opportunities and fundamentally shift how we think about employees, customers and the services we provide.

Can Others Do This and Why Bother?

With this essay then, I would like to challenge you to make an individual commitment to go back to your library and make just one change that will enhance social equity and empowerment. Change one instruction session, one handout, one exhibit or display, or reach out to one new group, advocate for collection policies that reflect socially responsible values, suggest changes to library access structures, or meet with a faculty member to discuss fair use and national information policies. You can do it, because we have done it. It is possible to act on your social values in this new environment. Libraries need social activists now more than ever.

Works Cited

ARL. *A Bimonthly Newsletter of Research Library Issues* (August 1998).

Berman, Sanford. *Prejudices and Antipathies: A Tract on the LC Subject Heads Concerning People.* Jefferson, NC: McFarland, 1993.

Piele, Linda J., and Brian Yamel. "Reference Assistance Project, University of Wisconsin–Parkside." *College and Research Library News* 3 (1982): 83–84.

Shera, Jesse. *Libraries and the Organization of Knowledge.* Hamden, CT: Archon, 1965.

Stoffle, Carla J. "The Emergence of Education and Knowledge Management as Major Functions of the Digital Library." Paper presented at the Follet Lecture Series. University of Wales. November 13, 1996.

_____. "Public Library Service to the Disadvantaged: A Bibliography, Part 1." *Library Journal* 94:1 (January 15,1969): 141–153. Part 2. *Library Journal* 94:1 (February 1, 1969): 507–515.

_____. "The Upside of Downsizing: Using the Economic Crisis to Structure and Revitalize Academic Libraries." In *The Upside of Downsizing: Using Library Instruction to Cope.* Comp. and ed. Cheryl LaGuardia. New York: Neal-Schuman, 1995.

_____, and Patricia E. Tarin. "A New Library for the New Undergraduate." *Library Journal* 115 (October 1, 1990): 47–51.

A Vicious Circle?

Barbara A. Bishop

Barbara A. Bishop received her M.A.L.S. from the University of South Florida in 1987. She has spent all of her professional career as a librarian at Auburn University where she is currently the government documents librarian. She has co-authored and has presented or co-presented papers on the history of the integration of the Alabama Library Association.

Librarians and social responsibility—seems like a perfect fit, doesn't it? You know you are socially responsible, don't you? After all, you support the Library Bill of Rights, you abhor censorship in any form and help any patron who comes to the desk no matter who they are or what they look like. You only have to look in any issue of *American Libraries* to find news briefs and letters about and by librarians who are of a like mind. But have you ever stopped to think that as a profession we are better at being socially responsible for our patrons' sakes than for our own? "NO!" you emphatically answer, "not me or my library." All right, let's stop and take a little unscientific poll.

The following questions were part of Christene Watkins's chapter report published a few years ago in *American Libraries*:

> Who do you see at your chapter's annual conference? Is the attendance more diverse than it was last year or five years ago? Does it reflect the mix of patrons at your library or other libraries you visit in your state? How does it compare to the mix of people you see on the bus or the freeway? At the grocery store or the local mall? At your children's school [9]?

Let's add two more questions to the poll. The number of patrons with differing ethnic backgrounds that your library serves has: a) gone up, b) gone down, c) remained unchanged. The number of librarians with differing ethnic backgrounds in your library has: a) gone up, b) gone down, c) remained unchanged.

For most people the answers to the last two questions would be "a" and "b" respectively. They certainly were at my library. The fact is that the library profession has a problem when it comes to recruiting, retaining, and promoting minority librarians. And it is not a new problem. I suspect that right about now many white librarians would deny this fact while many of the minority librarians would agree. Unfortunately, I also suspect that most of those who are reading this paper are already "in the choir."

It is not difficult to understand how librarians can be so progressive about external problems and so much less so about internal ones. The simplest answers are: it is easier to deal with external problems; we are being constantly reminded of them; and we have been working longer at them than at internal problems. It is an almost circular pattern because librarians have been indoctrinated for years to protect the rights of all readers. A book is challenged and the librarian responds to the challenge with mantra-like precision: with written policies, reference to the Bill of Rights, censorship issues, rights of all readers. A panel is convened, the challenge succeeds or fails. This established pattern becomes comfortable and therefore easier because it repeats over and over and over again.

How long have we been doing this? The American Library Association (ALA) established open membership in 1877, and one of the first major conferences dealing with access to libraries was in 1913. The Kaaterskill Conference, as it was called, mostly looked at the problems of service to disadvantaged groups. The association then organized Round Table on Work with Negroes in the early 1920s. By 1926, easy access to adequate library service for all was mentioned as a worthy goal in the publication *Library Extensions: A Study of Public Library Conditions and Needs.* The interesting thing about the latter two events is the naïvete of the participants in thinking that all the goals could be accomplished in just four or five years' time ("Institutional Membership," 369–70).

With the 1930s, two major actions by the association helped establish policy that would have ramifications for years to come. The first was in 1936 when, after a Richmond, Virginia, conference, ALA decided never to hold a meeting in a location that could not assure equal access to all its members. This resolution dealt only with the national organization and had no bearing on regional or state chapters. The second was the adoption of the first Library Bill of Rights in 1939. This version of the bill protected intellectual freedom regarding book selection and use of library meeting rooms but did not question the right of access to services ("Institutional Membership," 370–71).

Many of these compromises were probably reached because of the existing political and social differences among geographic regions. Also the thrust of the actions was to benefit the public rather than the profession. However, after the United States Supreme Court ruled in 1954 on *Brown v. Board of*

Education, the members of the association became much more attuned to the importance of politicizing and advocating change.

In 1954, the association decided not to hold a meeting in Miami Beach, Florida, because of the discrimination some of its members would face when they were denied equal access. It is this precedent that allows current ALA divisions the flexibility to move meetings whenever a city or state's laws or codes do not meet accepted ALA standards. Additionally, the association's amended constitution required each state chapter's bylaws to comply with the national bylaws by 1956, or the state associations would lose recognized chapter status. Because of city and state statutes neither the Alabama nor the Georgia chapter could comply with this condition, and they chose not to apply. Two other southern states, Louisiana and Mississippi, voluntarily withdrew their chapter status in 1963 ("Institutional Membership," 374).

Lest you immediately think: "Well, it's the South of course, they didn't want to comply," the recognized chapter for North Carolina came about by integrating two segregated associations in 1955–56 ("Institutional Membership," 374). The Alabama Library Association also attempted integration of its membership in the 1950s, but for many reasons this effort failed (Barrett, 141–61). It was not until after the passage of the Civil Rights Act of 1964 and much more political manipulation on ALA's part that these four states would comply and the American Library Association's list of chapters would be complete.

All this history helps to illustrate the point that librarians have been actively advocating for our users longer than we have for our profession. And here is a little more history. As you can imagine, the move toward equal access was not achieved without some divisiveness and strife. I think Patricia Glass Schuman said it best when she referred to the 1960s as a time of "angry optimism" which turned, in the 1970s, to "bewildered skepticism" (Schuman, "Social," 369). She collected many essays that appeared originally in *Library Journal* or *School Library Journal* between 1969 and 1976 and republished them in *Social Responsibilities and Libraries*. The subjects they covered included advocacy, service, women and minorities.

Several of the essays dealt with the recruitment, hiring and promotion of minority librarians. Mildred Dickeman, E. J. Josey, Patricia Schuman and Edward Mapp painted a pretty grim contemporary picture. Dickeman tackled the subject of institutional racism when she looked at how an institution's structure could result in discrimination (Dickeman, 96–102). Long a supporter of social change, Josey used statistics to demonstrate that libraries hired or promoted few minority librarians (Josey, 103–13). Schuman predicted the loss of all black librarians in the South because of overt and covert racism (Schuman, "Southern," 119–24). Despite his essay's discouraging title, "The Invisible Librarian," Mapp was the most optimistic in that he stressed some positive aspects of being a black librarian over the problems he had encountered or envisaged (Mapp, 114–18). All of the writers were cautiously optimistic.

You have probably figured out by now that the pessimism and "angry optimism" of these people existed because they were the ones "on the front lines." They had direct experience that many of us can now learn about by reading, listening to stories and asking questions of those who were in the trenches. Many of the original participants have since died, retired, or left the profession because of the backlash that ensued after the passage of the Civil Rights Act of 1964.

After a flurry of publishing in the late 1960s and early 1970s on and by ethnic minority librarians, the torrent of publications slowed to a trickle. It appeared that library administrators were falling in line with federal regulations in the recruiting and hiring of minorities. The problem was taking care of itself, right? Wrong! It would be far more correct to say rather that the problem had gone underground.

By the late 1980s, articles began to appear in library literature that revealed the dissatisfaction many minority librarians were feeling with the profession. In his 1988 piece "Yessuh! I's the Reference Librarian," Patrick A. Hall enumerated some of the problems he had encountered that made him an "invisible librarian" (Hall, 900–1). In 1992, the Black Caucus of ALA, founded in 1970, held the First National Conference of African American Librarians because "many black librarians are still dissatisfied with their treatment in ALA." Results of a telephone survey of minority librarians done by Evan St. Lifer and Corinne Nelson were published in 1997. This study discussed racism and discrimination in the library profession. Most recently Cynthia Preston published the results of a survey on discrimination, job satisfaction and minorities which indicates that racism and discrimination are currently two of the biggest concerns among many minority librarians.

Some common threads that run through these pieces are that the discrimination today is much more subtle than in years past, and that white experiences and perceptions are different from those of minorities. Explanations for both these trends can be described in terms of "comfort level." For example, minority librarians may be passed by at the reference desk because a patron feels more comfortable with a white librarian. Since the individual usually establishes his or her own comfort level, most white librarians do not perceive this type of discrimination. Please bear in mind that these are oversimplifications explaining complex social phenomena, but this does not make the explanations any less truthful.

A problem exists with the recruitment, retention and promotion of ethnic minorities in the library profession. E. J. Josey's work supports this conclusion. He used 1973 survey data collected by the American Library Association on the race of public library employees to demonstrate that the final makeup of white employees was over 93 percent, meaning that only 7 percent of all employees in public libraries were minorities (Josey, 104). The next ten years did see some improvement in the breakdowns but then stagnation ensued. By 1985 the figures for minorities had risen to Asians 3.4 percent, blacks 6.1 percent, Latinos 1.8 percent and whites 88.5 percent. But compare the 1985 figures to those of 1991: Asians 3.85 percent, blacks 6.28 percent, Latinos 1.8 percent, whites 87.7 percent (St. Lifer and Nelson, 42–46). As you can see there has been no appreciable growth in the number of ethnic minorities in fifteen years. Finally, previous to 1999, ALA had not kept figures by EEOC category; and although comparisons really cannot be made, the percentage of whites in the profession for both public and academic libraries is still over 86.5 percent (Lynch, 68).

There is an old saying that change begins at the top. While this is true, in this case change must occur within all of us as well. Read the current literature, especially the St. Lifer/Nelson and Preston articles, because they will probably shock you. I can remember, while doing research on the integration issues of libraries in Alabama, that my writing partner and I were amazed at some of the horrific incidents and stories of overt discrimination we uncovered. Until researching this essay, I had never really looked at the profession. Afterwards I saw some of the same incidents recurring. I was complacent in my position because they were not happening to me.

Becoming aware of a problem is usually the first step in resolving it, but hard work and time are also part of the solution. The problems faced by minority librarians are emotionally charged because they strike close to the cultural core of our existence. By looking at the history we are able to get to the root of the problem without becoming defensive and assigning blame. This history also illustrates that when librarians acknowledge a problem they can resolve it using a variety of methods.

Also, do not make the mistake of thinking this is not your problem because "we don't have any minorities." That argument is old and tired. I remember giving a talk on the Americans with Disabilities Act at a rather upscale public library where the director said: "I don't understand why we have to comply. After all, we don't have any handicapped people who come here." Someone pointed out to her that the bicycle rack she had placed in the parking lot blocked the curb possibly projecting a message that the handicapped are not welcome here.

Are we sending this message to our own? Recruiting into librarianship is hard regardless of race, especially in today's market. Many of us did not set out to become librarians. We sort of stumbled into it or chose it as a second profession. Compound that with the fact that currently the economy is so good that people with bachelor's degrees often have higher starting salaries than librarians, who must have master's level education. Perhaps another factor contributing to the dearth of minority candidates is that individual libraries do not actively recruit them. The "women and minorities welcome to apply" message is commonplace, but it may be nothing more than lip service. Who would accept a position in which a timid "please apply" invitation is overshadowed by a subliminal "you're not welcome" one? This may then perpetuate a situation where people who might be interested in the profession hesitate because they see so few minority role models to encourage them to enter.

The subject of role models leads me to another point. An administrator's job is just beginning after a minority librarian is hired. One frequently cited problem throughout the literature is the lack of mentors for newly hired minority librarians. In some cases, the administrator needs to go even further by helping the successful candidate become aware of a community's minority network. Judith Castiano, a member of ALA's Reforma, has spoken about her first attempt to get a library degree. She said that she left Illinois after a month because, in addition to being away from home, no one looked like her (Watkins, 9). Being hooked into the Latino community may not have changed Castiano's decision to return home, but it could at least have given her an alternative viewpoint.

As Kathleen de la Peña McCook points out, the number of committees to which a minority librarian is assigned can be overwhelming. She notes that too much committee work does not leave enough time for the research and publishing that are prerequisites for success in the university (Watkins, 9). In trying to do the right thing—i.e., making sure that minorities are represented on committees—the administrator making the assignments inadvertently sabotages the candidate's chances at tenure. This, of course, compounds the original problem.

It seems like a vicious circle, doesn't it? Well, it is in some ways. Additionally, we must accept the fact that there will be no single, easy solution. But ALA, several state organizations, and many minority librarians are already creating the paths for us to follow. You help by becoming aware of the problem, educating and sensitizing yourself and constantly reassessing your viewpoints. In this way you have made the first step towards indoctrinating the next generation to the "mantra-like precision" needed to tackle this problem. They will in turn educate the next generation, which will educate the next, until the internal problems of racism are addressed with the same consciousness that informs our response to the problems of our patrons.

Works Cited

Barrett, Kayla, and Barbara A. Bishop. "Integration and the Alabama Library Association: Not So Black and White." *Libraries & Culture* 33 (1998): 141–61.

Dickeman, Mildred. "Racism in the Library: A Model from the Public Schools." *Social Responsibilities and Libraries*. Comp. and ed. Patricia Glass Schuman. New York: R. R. Bowker, 1976: 96–102

Hall Patrick A. "Yessuh! I's the Reference Librarian." *American Libraries* Nov. 1988: 900–901. Expanded Academic ASAP. Ralph Brown Draughon Library, Auburn, AL. 13 Feb. 1999 (http://web2.searchbank.com/).

"Institutional Membership in ALA," *ALA Bulletin* April 1966: 362–374.

Josey, E. J. "Can Library Affirmative Action Succeed?" *Social Responsibilities and Libraries*. Comp. and ed. Patricia Glass Schuman. New York: R. R. Bowker, 1976: 103–13.

Lynch, Mary Jo. "Librarians' Salaries: Smaller Increases This Year." *American Libraries* (Nov. 1998): 68.

Mapp, Edward. "The Invisible Librarian." *Social Responsibilities and Libraries*. Comp. and ed. Patricia Glass Schuman. New York: R. R. Bowker, 1976: 114–118.

Nelson, Corinne O. "Unity Through Diversity: A Call to Work." *Library Journal* (1 Oct. 1994): 38–41. Expanded Academic ASAP. Ralph Brown Draughon Library, Auburn, AL. 9 Feb. 1999 (http://web2.searchbank.com/).

Preston, Cynthia. "Perceptions of Discriminatory Practices and Attitudes: A Survey of African American Librarians." *College & Research Libraries* (Sept. 1998): 434–45.

St. Lifer, Evan, and Corinne Nelson. "Unequal Opportunities: Race Does Matter." *Library Journal* (1 Nov. 1997): 42–6. Expanded Academic ASAP. Ralph Brown Draughon Library, Auburn, AL. 13 Feb. 1999. (http://web2.searchbank.com/).

Schuman, Patricia Glass. "Social Responsibility: An Agenda for the Future." *Social Responsibilities and Libraries*. Comp. and ed. Patricia Glass Schuman. New York: R. R. Bowker, 1976: 369–77.

_____. "Southern Integration: Writing Off the Black Librarian." *Social Responsibilities and Libraries*. Comp. and ed. Patricia Glass Schuman. New York: R. R. Bowker, 1976: 119–24.

Watkins, Christene. "Chapter Report: Going to the Sources—Recruiting for Diversity." *American Libraries*. August 1996: 9. Academic Search Elite. Ralph Brown Draughon Library, Auburn, AL. 9 Feb. 1999 (http://www.epnet.com/ehost/login.html).

Fish Out of Water

Marie Jones

Marie F. Jones is currently working as the Extended Campus Librarian at East Tennessee State University, Johnson City, Tennessee. Previously, she was reference and bibliographic instruction librarian at Muskingum College in New Concord, Ohio, since 1990. She is the general editor of Annotations: A Guide to the Independent Critical Press *(Baltimore: Alternative Press Center, 1999).*

I'm not entirely sure why I'm here. I'm not a heroic librarian facing the world's ills with an activist's courage and strength, demonstrating, fighting, going all out for the causes I care about. Neither am I a big fish in the library world. I am a reference and bibliographic instruction librarian at a small midwestern liberal arts college. I'm a very small fish in a very small pond.

Still, I have the idealistic notion that with enough small fish flapping their tails, we can make waves. There was a time in my life when I wanted desperately to work at a left-leaning college. To work with colleagues that shared my politics in an institution that supported my activism seemed my dream situation. But I've come to think that more good may be done as part of a minority, gently nudging from within a conservative institution.

Over the course of nearly a decade, I've seen a few individuals do great things for our campus. Various faculty, staff, students, and alums have revitalized the Women's Center; they have helped the few minority students to work together as a group; they have begun a strong gay/les/bi group; they have provided opportunities for first year students who might become future campus leaders to work with the homeless and to gain insight into issues of poverty; and they have contributed a collection to the library of gay and lesbian studies materials. I haven't been involved in any of these actions. I'm merely a bystander to most, applauding and encouraging those who are doing the real work. But, even by standing at the sidelines I hope I'm making an impact. If

118

a person like me, shyer or more cautious than the leaders on campus, can help provide an atmosphere where it's okay to be a real activist, then I've flapped my fish tail in a helpful way.

How do I know that? Once upon a time, I was an 18-year-old conservative small town truck driver's daughter. I left my little town and went to college, seeing my only other options as marriage or working at the five-and-dime. I chose a small, midwestern church-affiliated liberal arts college not unlike my current institution. At that college, I encountered discussions of class and gender that gave me a new perspective on my home life, and my place at this private school. I discovered writings by women of color with whom I identified more thoroughly than any other writers I'd ever encountered. I learned that the church could not just amplify injustice but work for social justice as well. I also found that people I respected had views different from folks back home. They didn't proselytize, but shared their views, and over time I came to adopt some of them as my own.

So now as an adult, I try always to be who I am, in and out of the library and classroom. I am a person with beliefs, with a worldview different from many of my students and much of the faculty. It would be easy to take on whatever social mantle is nearby, to "dress for success" in word and deed. I try not to. I believe in causes of social justice. I am a feminist. I am an environmentalist. I am a vegetarian. This makes me eccentric in my world but I don't think I'm so far off the mark that students can't identify with me.

How do the students even know these things about me? It's not that I blurt out my philosophy of life every time someone stops at the reference desk to ask directions to the bathroom. I don't share these beliefs in the middle of the basic reference interview. It wouldn't do any good if I did. Students have to trust me before they can learn anything about life from me; I have to trust them before I reveal too much of myself to them. Sometimes, though, they know because they ask. I dress funny. I eat funny. Organic clothing isn't exactly de rigeur for the average librarian in New Concord. Vegetarianism as an environmental and feminist act is unheard of. If a student in a class asks, I tell her that I do these things because I try to live lightly on the land. Some dismiss me as a nutcase; others ask more questions. Maybe some of the deeper questioners will go on to be real activists. Or, perhaps, little fish, like me, flapping.

Unfortunately, I flap less and less effectively in the institution of the library itself. I can point students in the direction of alternative resources, but I don't have much control over how many alternatives are available. I can do my research in the field of alternative press serials, and I can suggest titles to students who are researching in applicable areas, but the materials aren't immediately accessible to them. They have to order them through interlibrary loan because we don't have subscriptions to those titles. I feel most powerless here, because it is here that I should be able to make a difference.

Libraries need to provide a broad range of materials to have a balanced collection, including alternative viewpoints from alternative publishers. This I firmly believe. But how does a librarian without collection development responsibilities affect change in the collection as a whole? And how, with a tiny reference budget, can I afford to purchase more than a few materials outside of the mainstream or representing alternative viewpoints? I frankly don't know. I can only hope that being aware of the alternatives will help me direct students outside of our collection, and that they will use the few items I have purchased.

I also hope that by working on my students' critical thinking and information literacy skills, I can help them to choose their own battles and their own ethical stances more wisely. If I can teach even one student to question the media diet she lives on daily, I will have made a worthwhile contribution.

Flap. So here I am. Trying in the face of the dampening influences of daily life to make a difference in the world. Not a big difference. Just what I can do. Sometimes I feel guilty that I don't do more. I could risk my comfort and be more of a real activist. But somehow I don't feel like that's my place in the world. Then again, maybe my flapping tail is where my revolution resides.

Frameworks: The Poetics of Libraries

Nancy Kuhl

Nancy Kuhl is the author of In the Arbor, *a collection of poems published by Kent State University Press. Her work has appeared in* Cream City Review, Poetry Northwest, Puerto del Sol, Quarter After Eight, *and other journals.*

SUNY at Buffalo's main library, Lockwood Memorial Library, is a strange building, built semi-pentagonally around a stone walkway and a sunken courtyard. From the reference desk, which is on the building's second floor, one sees three stories of windows rising on all sides of the yard. Below: the pale, six-sided bricks that make up the patio floor, a cluster of slender pine trees, benches. In truth, the courtyard isn't welcoming or appealing. If I stand in the yard's center, I am basement level and five stories of windows rise on every side. Only a swatch of sky is visible, and that seems oddly distant and vague. On clear days, the courtyard is in almost constant shade; when it's overcast, the gray is enhanced, made somehow larger and more palpable. Everything visible from the window seems taut, ordered; the rows of windows, the perfectly circular tables, the courtyard rail—three slender metal bars, horizontal, crossed by periodic verticals, like a rail fence pared down to its bare bones. Even the pine trees seem only to have been included for their form, their narrow, vertical trunks, their sloping branches.

I work at the reference desk in Lockwood; as a graduate student in the University at Buffalo's School of Information Studies, I've been given the opportunity to work here as an intern, answering basic reference questions. Late morning, last Tuesday, I found the reference area unusually quiet. The sun, which we had not seen in many dull and snowy days, was finally shining. The library was nearly empty. Through the library's windows, sunlight on snow in the courtyard took on a peculiar quality, dense and heavy. The windows across the courtyard reflected the light back in flat sheets.

Because there were few patron questions to address, I took advantage of the opportunity to familiarize myself with a new full text database of newspaper and magazine articles. My practice search was for information about a favorite play, *Six Degrees of Separation*. Uncertain about how the search system worked, I decided on a broad search first; I input only the name of the author, John Guare, to see what sort of results I'd get. My inexpert practice search retrieved too many hits to wade through; I decided to abandon the results and begin again.

But as I clicked the browser "back" button, something caught my attention. The artist Chuck Close, whose enormous portraits fascinate me, was mentioned in the second citation. I returned to my search results and found the citation for a review of a book about Close for young readers called *Chuck Close, Up Close* (the record was retrieved because the review mentions Guare's own book about Close, *Chuck Close: Life and Work 1995–1998*). I am enrolled in a young adult library services class which requires that I read a number of non-fiction titles. I logged out of the database, consulted the online catalog. The book was in Lockwood, in the basement, two floors below. From the windows in the reference area, I could just make out the shadowy shape of the stacks through the windows that face the courtyard.

My clumsy search led me to a beautiful little book filled with color photos of Close's work. Some of Close's giant portraits look, at first, like wild, patternless arrangements of color. When you step back you begin to see the form, the structure, the shape of human features. The face emerges from the blocks of blue and orange and gold. The organization and form aren't clear when viewed at close range, though the blur of colors is lovely. One must step back and look again. A woman's face, framed by dark curly hair, eyes green as the sea.

The book includes a photo of Close's 1997 *Self Portrait* in progress. Close's forehead, his eyes and nose are visible. The lower half of his face is, as yet, little more than squares of color. Close paints from photographs, which he breaks into grids. He translates the image from each grid to its corresponding space in the painting. In the finished portrait, the solid squares become the structure upon which the image builds. Each square is complicated by more colors, more shades, interior circles, ovals, lines. Take just one small square: the center is a red dot, an imprecise form surrounded by pink, more red, orange, bright green. The purple-gray edges of the square line up with still more color, more squares and rectangles, pale blue, yellow, gold, more pink, more orange.

Faced with Close's portraits, it takes a moment to be sure what one is looking at. In the seconds before the face emerges, the blocks of color seem at once arbitrary and purposeful. The eyes show themselves first, come into focus as centers of both light and dark, places on the canvas where white, black, deep blue or green or brown dominate. I am transfixed by the eyes, which do not look like another's eyes, but like what I might see if I could look closely enough, if I could look this closely at my own eyes.

Just a few weeks into my first semester in the masters' of library science program, I found myself thinking frequently about what library innovator Charles Ammi Cutter referred to as the syndetic structure of the library. When I think of the structure created by a catalog and classification system, I think of a stained-glass window, translucent chips of green and blue, their edges clearly defined by dark metal veins. Everything is held in place, yet light makes the arrangement fluid, shifting, evolving as day moves to dusk and to dark.

The structures which organize the library are suggestive, implying relationships—be they figurative, linguistic, historic, cultural—between and among seemingly unrelated subjects. Opening the so-called Red Books, the Library of Congress Subject Headings, Volume IV, N–R at random, I find the following terms sharing a page: Quadrille (dance); Quadrille (game); Quadriplegics; Quadroons—use Mulattoes; Quadrula Fragosa—use Winged Maple Leaf (mollusk). The terms on this page, and their associated concepts, tumble in a semi-confusion of sound and shape. The terms are linguistically related in obvious ways, sharing the prefix *quad*, meaning four, and sharing the sounds of their common letters.

The associations among the words are expanded, however, simply by the fact that they inhabit common space in the Red Books. These additional associations are imagined, perhaps, or intuited, but they exist nonetheless. In part, their relationships are a function of the fact that they exist in this book, as classifiers, terms humans select to define the things and people that populate the world around them. We can name and define a quadrille (dance) and thus know it apart from a Quadrula Fragosa. We slide people into categories—quadriplegic, crippled, disabled, physically challenged; quadroon, mulatto, black, white, yellow. We use language to define everything around us and the language itself suggests and creates connections where they were never intended.

These suggested relationships have an impact on the way one thinks, on how one constructs research questions, and on how one approaches the library catalog. The controlled subject headings determine the universe of knowledge, instruct us as to what is possible. Turning again to the Red Books, I find Posture in Art just above Posture in Worship. My mind calls up images from paintings of martyred saints, a woman on her knees, a man whose shoulders are bent like the curved underside of a bridge. I remember stained glass portraits of the holy family, Joseph standing behind Mary who cradles the infant, searching his face. Instead of considering each heading separately, the two bleed together easily, become one.

Thus, the associations and relationships created by the language of the Red Books, in effect, define a tremendous, nearly limitless potential for what can be or might be known. Even the colloquial name of the Library of Congress Subject Headings, the Red Books, is suggestive of some potency, some mythic or magic quality, as though they were books of spells in a fairy tale, as though these pages might reveal a method of changing iron to gold. And they do (do they not?) act as a contained map, a kind of composite of the library, the universe of knowledge, the world as we know it. The Red Books call to mind the etymology of the word *text*, from the Latin for *woven*. Their structure, like that of a spider's web, spinning outward strand after strand, knits and connects—words, ideas, names, languages. Quadrille (dance); Quadrula Fragosa—use Winged Maple Leaf (mollusk).

The library's system of connectedness provides a structure that, in some ways, is not unlike the structure of metaphor or rhyme in poetry. There is an implied relationship between two words that rhyme; their shared sounds give us the sense that their meanings are connected as well. One need only think of some of our culture's favorite (albeit clichéd) rhymes to see how effectively rhymes connect words and how lasting that connection can be in the human consciousness—take love and dove, for instance, or moon, spoon, and June.

In poetry we talk about sound relationships with the terms *rhyme* and *assonance* and *consonance*. In psychological word association tests, the same phenomenon of language is referred to as *clang association*. Whichever terms you prefer, the idea is consistent: we associate words together based on common elements, and we make meaningful relationship between the concepts these words represent where they might not otherwise exist.

The syndetic structure of the library, this matrix of language and ideas, generates a kind of poetics of the library, one that allows us to envision possibilities and make the kind of intuitive connections that language allows us to make in poetry.

UB's Poetry/Rare Books Collection has an enormous reading room, the walls of which are lined with display cases and hung with remarkable paintings—primarily portraits of writers: William Carlos Williams, Dylan Thomas, Wyndham Lewis. A portrait of James Joyce hangs not far from a case displaying several of his canes, his passport, and the lenses from his eyeglasses. The portrait is traditional, representational, the sort of portrait one might commission. Joyce is wearing a red necktie, a pale suit jacket, and the round glasses that are now in the display case.

I've been working at the Poetry/Rare Books Collection for about six months. As I enter at the start of each shift, I find generally the same scene: two or three of the long tables in the reading room are covered with books, manuscript boxes, notes. Scholars sit here, often for many hours, hunched shoulders bent toward their work. Many return frequently, even from distant cities, and know all of us who work in the library by name.

The Poetry/Rare Books Collection shares its reading room with the University Archives. Sometimes, I enter the room to find a professor or student examining some unusual object from the archives, some human artifact whose particular significance to the university cannot be ascertained from a distance: a vase, a scrapbook, an American flag. Not long ago, I watched the university archivist and a person from the libraries' preservation department spread long, loosely woven, orange-gold curtains on a reading table, trying to determine the best way to store the pieces.

Thinking back to those curtains, their texture and uneven surface, their place in the university's collections, I am reminded of Close's portraits and the way organization supports individual, seemingly unrelated pieces of a whole. The pieces—monographs, recordings, artifacts—in a library collection are held in relational positions by the systems that structure the library, from subject headings and archival finding aids to the physical shelves, bookplates, and the boxes and wrappers that protect rare and fragile materials.

These structures help to create equivalents among library holdings. Things become alike simply by being part of the same collection; their value is inherent in the fact that, for whatever reason, they have been deemed worthy of being collected, cared for, preserved. The University at Buffalo libraries contain widely diverse pieces, many of which are unique and seem entirely unrelated to the collection as a whole, a collection which, like any research institution's, takes scholarship as its primary goal. Take, for example, the following: The Kelley Collection of Pulp Fiction; an extensive collection of "zines"—independently produced magazines, often photocopied, stapled, even hand colored; rare first editions of important literary works, including a signed first edition of Nathaniel Hawthorne's *The Scarlet Letter*; a painting by the poet e.e. cummings; a mask made for Katharine Cornell, the early twentieth-century stage actress known as "the First Lady of the Theatre."

William Carlos Williams's desk is in a corner of a small room off the reading room at the Poetry/Rare Books Collection, where the collections' reference materials are shelved. It is an unusual desk, with a built in typewriter that can be stored underneath when not in use, leaving a plain desktop. Williams, a poet and physician, would flip the typewriter up between patient visits to his home office. He wrote then, working on poems in what time he had among the day's appointments. He stored the typewriter when his patients were in the office, looking at them, I imagine, across the flat surface concealing the typewriter and his poems.

These distinctly different artifacts and texts, when collected together create a particular record of humanity, one with implications far beyond what each monograph or serial or object might signify independently. A library's collection is a collage of the culture it represents. And as in any collage, the meanings of individual pieces combine to create something more. The relationship of one thing to another—a scrap of newspaper, a bit of green cloth, fat blue brush strokes—generates an entirely new image or narrative; out of this assortment of pieces appears the image of a violin or a glass of wine on a café table. Libraries collect, organize, and preserve materials of the cultural record, and their collections can tell us who we have been and who we are. Without such a record, what can we know? How can we create new knowledge without an understanding of the complicated human context in which we exist?

Still no collection, however vast and complete, can provide an absolute picture of the culture from which it has been gleaned. The Poetry/Rare Books Collection has been collecting poetry in English for nearly a century. There is, perhaps, no more complete collection of contemporary poetry in English anywhere in the world. And yet, if one read every book in this library, she wouldn't know everything there is to know about contemporary poetry in English. Reading every book, studying every artifact in the university's libraries, one would gain only an incomplete understanding of the human culture the collections stand for.

There is a story about a man who wanted to know the weight of smoke. Unable to collect and measure the elusive substance, the man instead weighed a cigar, smoked it, weighed the ash that remained and determined that the difference was the weight of the smoke. There is a kind of logic to the equation: cigar = ash + smoke. And yet, we know that the hypothesis is flawed and will not reveal the weight of the smoke that curls from the cigar or from the smoker's open mouth. Things do not always add up, revealing a unified whole.

Books, relics, works of art are records of human endeavor, achievement, and knowledge, but they are only part of the story. The UB Libraries' collection, indeed any library's collection, can provide only a framework on which to hang theory, idea, interpretation, advancement, judgment, imagination.

Before I started working at the Poetry/Rare Books Collection, I wondered about the wisdom of keeping the bulk of the University libraries' poetry in closed stacks. As an undergraduate, I started seriously reading poetry by browsing the stacks in my university's library. I often sat on the floor for hours, pulling books haphazardly, reading a poem or two, until I found a book that compelled me to read it through. Rarely could I have told anyone what I was looking for as I read around in those books; it would have been impossible for me to locate the very book I wanted in the catalog so that a librarian or clerk could retrieve it from closed stacks. I recognized, of course, the need to protect fragile and rare materials, but I feared that the poetry collection might be an elitist endeavor, keeping all poetry (not just books considered rare or unique) out of the hands of all but the most committed scholars. Since poetry is traditionally an oral art form, it seemed possible that such a collection would rarefy poetry, sapping it of much of its energy as a spoken, communal art form.

But there is a difference between imagining a library collection and walking through a library's stacks; likewise, there is a difference between recognizing that libraries serve a preservation function and understanding the ends such a function serves. The idea is somewhat static; the thing itself is dynamic. Walking through the closed stacks at the Poetry/Rare Books Collection for the first time, it became clear to me that the value of preservation is preservation itself. It is not a means to an end, but an end in and of itself. There is something vibrant in the collection, a sense that this is a growing component and record of an expansive and expanding culture.

On my third day working at the Poetry/Rare Books Collection, I accompanied the associate curator to the vault. Listening as he dialed the combination (I was self-conscious enough to look away, ensuring I wouldn't inadvertently see the correct numbers), I felt like I was in some kind of bizarre spy film. Inside the giant metal door, however, were mundane shelves stacked with gray cardboard manuscript boxes. Black metal file cabinets stood on either side of the doorway. The inside of the vault looked remarkably like the outside of the vault.

Of course, looks deceive. That day I held manuscript pages of Walt Whitman's work, handwritten drafts of his poems. It sounds clichéd and banal— me, a star-struck student, new to the library profession, encountering this unique text, this most important and rare document. But standing among books and papers, with the pages in my hands, I considered the sloping script and it was not banal. Some past owner had bound the pages in tooled leather; it looks like many other books. It does not reveal itself. I felt the particular weight of that particular book; my finger traced the spine. I don't know how to keep this scene from becoming just some piece of a library testimonial (one can hear it already, "and *this*, this moment, is why I became a librarian…"). I don't know how to describe the pages so that their precise texture, smooth and dense, will seem real.

I can't say why such an experience should feel like a revelation, and yet I am not alone in this. There is an epiphanic quality in many human meetings with the relics of our cultural past. In his essay, "Unpacking My Library," the philosopher Walter Benjamin notes that when one looks upon artifacts, "he seems to be seeing through them into their distant past as though inspired." An artifact's existence alone teaches us something. "The acquisition of an old book," Benjamin tells us, "is its rebirth." The book is reborn to us when we encounter its first incarnation, no matter how many editions it has passed through.

The preservation and collection functions of libraries are essential, more now, perhaps, than at any time in the past. In a culture which attaches more and more value to multimedia, non-book materials, the collection and preservation of rare and ordinary books reminds us of their inherent value as resources and as artifacts. A poetry collection such as UB's represents a (relatively) small but vital piece of poetry's (and humankind's) history; it is a unique and essential cultural record. Its very existence affirms the lasting importance of poetry and humanity's perpetual commitment to this art across time and culture.

When we encounter pieces of humanity's history, we recognize pieces of our own lives in them, our own successes and failures, our own mortality. Katharine Cornell, the stage actress, died in 1974 and yet her stage mask, stored in the Poetry/Rare Books Collection, captures perfectly the cast of her face. The actress's face, its singular shape and form, is gone from the world; the mask remains, and I can hold it to my own face, see through its oval eye holes. Like the traveler in Shelley's "Ozymandias," who encounters a fallen statue of an ancient king, we know that the passions that drove both sculptor and king "yet survive." They drive us still.

Yesterday, working at the reference desk at Lockwood, a woman asked for my assistance finding a dissertation her professor had encouraged her to read.

"The title is *Literature or Theory Review*," she said. Her heavy German accent was difficult for me to understand and the question seemed unclear: was the title *Literature* or *Theory Review* or *Literature or Theory Review*? None seemed likely dissertation titles.

"Do you know the author's name? Or the academic department the dissertation was written for?"

She did: William Anderson, Sociology. The title seemed even more unlikely with the addition of this information. A search for the author's name turned up several possibilities, only one from the Sociology department. But the title, which was a long and complicated one, didn't include the words Literature or Theory or Review.

"Is it possible you've got the title wrong? Or that your professor misremembered it?" I asked.

"No. It isn't possible. Please look again," she replied, clearly frustrated by my inability to produce a call number.

I tried another search in the library's catalog, finding only the same title. I searched a database of dissertation abstracts and still couldn't find anything different. It was near the end of my four-hour shift at the desk, I was tired, and I wondered if the problem was me, my inexperience, my fatigue. Perhaps, somewhere along the line, I had misunderstood the woman's request.

I asked the woman if she could tell me something about the dissertation's subject matter. She couldn't. I suggested we might be able to locate another source that would help her, if she would tell me more about the kinds of information she was looking for. She wouldn't. I felt like I'd exhausted all my options.

My training for this internship was extensive; it included a great deal of discussion and reading about the so-called "reference interview," the process by which librarians attempt to understand a library user's question and determine what source or sources will satisfy the need. The process is also known as the "reference negotiation," and the term is an accurate one. It is a process of give and take, trial and error, coaxing details from a broad request. And the coaxing continues when one approaches a catalog or database; one enters set after set of terms, keywords, subject headings, looking for the best match of word and concept. Because our language is rich with synonyms, free association is a necessity. And, unfortunately, reference negotiations are not always successful.

"Perhaps you could ask your professor for the title again, to confirm that this isn't the right dissertation." I scrawled the call number of the dissertation that matched the author and academic department. "Or maybe you could find this dissertation by William Anderson and try to figure out if it's the one your professor mentioned."

Without replying, the woman left. She stormed off really, and I was left feeling terrible, like a failure and a lousy excuse for a librarian.

A friend asked me why some books of poetry are assigned subject headings and others are not. He asked if there is a system by which catalogers determine which books of poetry will receive these designators and which won't. I have asked a few people, librarians who it seemed to me ought to know. None had a straight answer; each gave vague replies about copy cataloging or cataloger subjectivity. There is, perhaps, no good explanation why some books of poetry have no subject headings, while other are blessed with such combinations as Earthquakes—California—Poetry, and AIDS—Patients—Treatment—Poetry. Poetry is a free-floating subdivision in the Library of Congress Subject Headings; conceivably, it could be attached to any other heading: Fathers and Daughters—Poetry; Biology—Poetry; Lunar Eclipses—Poetry.

Coordinating subject headings allows one to conflate ideas. And what is built when subject headings are combined is more than just a new subject; the combining of terms is imaginative work resulting in fantastic potentialities. Custer, George Armstrong, 1839–1876—Poetry; Barbie Dolls—Poetry. Subject headings are combined to name complicated caprice: Library Science—Poetry; Blackberries—Poetry; Afro-American Women—United States—Crimes Against—Poetry. The language strings braid concepts together, creating not new concepts, exactly, but complex, multifaceted representations of one's most mundane thoughts or ideas.

Even individually, before they've been coordinated into particular headings for particular pieces, the array of subject terms is astonishing. The heading Perfumes has terms like Perfumery, Scented Books, and Perfume Bottles stacked up above and Cosmetics, Odors, and Toilet Preparations strung below. As I've described it, this chain of terms doesn't account for the likely sub-headings by geographic or chronological divisions or the fact that the term splits in two very different directions: Perfumes: manners and customs, and Perfumes: chemical technology. The term contains seemingly innumerable possibilities—and perfume-related and -derivative terms cover only a few inches of one column in the Red Books. A larger conceptual term will explode into greater possibilities: terms dealing with aspects of psychology, for instance, cover about ten pages.

I once spent an entire shift at the Poetry/Rare Books Collection photo-copying letters the poet Robert Duncan wrote to his companion, the artist known simply as Jess. I couldn't read much of the letters, of course, as I copied them, mostly just the greetings and salutations. One other thing I noticed about the letters: in the margins of nearly every letter, Duncan noted his traveling expenses: $1.50 for coffee and doughnut; $3.00 cab fare. The numbers, scribbled alongside the text, seem like a separate record, somehow only accidentally included. Hotel room rates, meal costs (including tip), laundry fees, the price of a new jacket. Some of the envelopes are stuffed with receipts.

I wonder about those margin notes and about what they might mean about Duncan and about Jess. I wonder if Duncan was neurotic about money or if Jess kept him on a short financial leash. The truth, I suspect, is less gossipy, but somehow more interesting—they were struggling, perhaps, an artist and a poet, trying to build a life. I don't know much about Duncan; I've read only a few of his poems. From where I stood copying the letters, I could take a step back, turn to my left and face Jess's heavily-textured painting of Duncan, standing in an ordinary, if brightly golden, room. There is a black cat at his feet; the cat embodies an explosive energy, looks about to leap. In his poem "Often I Am Permitted to Return to a Meadow," I can suppose that the library is a meadow we are permitted to return to, a place that is and is not ours. In the case of Duncan's letters at the Poetry/Rare Books Collection, we are permitted to enter fields within fields: we enter as Duncan, who writes the letters, and as Jess who reads them. We enter as witness to their lives as they appear in text and in image.

In the painting, Duncan is holding a book in his right hand, resting his left hand on the back of a chair. The hands, really, are just a few broad brush-strokes—pink, green-gray, white. They are the unmistakable impression of hands, holding a book, resting on a chair back. Below the right wrist, paint seems to pile up, the texture becomes uneven. The paint creates a three-dimensional surface, with craters, raised seams, defined brushstrokes. In some places, the paint has dripped, leaving imprecise trails of color over color, violet over red.

Individually, the brushstrokes, like the margin notes, say nothing. It is their combined weight that holds my attention. Cumulatively they become something, a narrative, an impression. Cumulatively they represent a life, two lives. The Poetry/Rare Books Collection holds an extensive collection of work by both Jess and Robert Duncan—Duncan's poems and manuscripts, exhibit catalogs from Jess's shows, pages and books lining shelves, spines announcing titles that tell only pieces of the story.

There are boxes and boxes of Duncan's letters. A scholar writing a biography of the poet has asked us to copy all of them. It will take days.

Nostalgia and revelation are at the root of collecting. One gathers things—books, artifacts—for the dual purpose of remembering what has been and creating what will be. Library collections allow humankind to invent its own future by example. A library's holdings are a collection of examples of human life, knowledge, association. We collect what means something to us, what we admire, love, fear. Any collection, whether it holds books of poems or antique furniture, announces itself as an example of how we see ourselves, what we envision is still to come, how we imagine our past.

This is human culture bearing witness to itself. In library collections the past exists in the present and the present exists into the future. We develop collections even though we know that their incompleteness is inevitable. Their report of the past they represent will be inexact. It will be a photo just out of focus, a defined shape whose details are visible but unclear. We recognize the impossibility of collecting everything of value and importance and we continue collecting, organizing, cataloging, naming.

The systems we employ to organize and make sense of the things we gather, systems of classification, uniform headings, related terms and headings, these too are only outlines, promising an outside chance, the hope of containing and controlling that which we know is finally beyond our control. The Library of Congress issues new Red Books every year, because there are ever more terms, more fields, more small universes of knowledge.

Structure communicates just one component of the whole. Chuck Close's portraits are not conventional representations; they are examples of a way one might see another's face. The facial geometry of these portraits conceals and reveals the human face's familiar structure. Each square of color brings the image closer to focus. The face, foreign and familiar, remembers and reveals almost everything. We look, then look more closely. What we are and what we are not is there. Most of it. Almost everything worth saving or naming is right here, just where we thought it would be.

Index